THE
HISTORY OF
PANAMA

THE
HISTORY OF
PANAMA

Robert C. Harding

The Greenwood Histories of the Modern Nations
Frank W. Thackeray and John E. Findling, Series Editors

Greenwood Press
Westport, Connecticut • London

Library of Congress Cataloging-in-Publication Data

Harding, Robert C.
    The history of Panama / Robert C. Harding.
        p. cm. — (The Greenwood histories of the modern nations; 1096–2905)
    Includes bibliographical references and index.
    ISBN 0–313–33322–X
      1. Panama—History.   I. Title.   II. Series.
  F1566.H37   2006
  972.87—dc22   2006001176

British Library Cataloguing in Publication Data is available.

Library of Congress Catalog Card Number: 2006001176
ISBN: 0–313–33322–X
ISSN: 1096–2905

First published in 2006

Greenwood Press, 88 Post Road West, Westport, CT 06881
An imprint of Greenwood Publishing Group, Inc.
www.greenwood.com

Printed in the United States of America

The paper used in this book complies with the
Permanent Paper Standard issued by the National
Information Standards Organization (Z39.48–1984).

10 9 8 7 6 5 4 3 2 1

Contents

Series Foreword

The *Greenwood Histories of the Modern Nations* series is intended to provide students and interested laypeople with up-to-date, concise, and analytical histories of many of the nations of the contemporary world. Not since the 1960s has there been a systematic attempt to publish a series of national histories, and, as editors, we believe that this series will prove to be a valuable contribution to our understanding of other countries in our increasingly interdependent world.

Over thirty years ago, at the end of the 1960s, the Cold War was an accepted reality of global politics, the process of decolonization was still in progress, the idea of a unified Europe with a single currency was unheard of, the United States was mired in a war in Vietnam, and the economic boom of Asia was still years in the future. Richard Nixon was president of the United States, Mao Tse-tung (not yet Mao Zedong) ruled China, Leonid Brezhnev guided the Soviet Union, and Harold Wilson was prime minister of the United Kingdom. Authoritarian dictators still ruled most of Latin America, the Middle East was reeling in the wake of the Six-Day War, and Shah Reza Pahlavi was at the height of his power in Iran. Clearly, the past 30 years have been witness to a great deal of historical change, and it is to this change that this series is primarily addressed.

With the help of a distinguished advisory board, we have selected nations whose political, economic, and social affairs mark them as among the most important in the waning years of the twentieth century, and for each nation we have found an author who is recognized as a specialist in the history of that nation. These authors have worked most cooperatively with us and with Greenwood Press to produce volumes that reflect current research on their nations and that are interesting and informative to their prospective readers.

The importance of a series such as this cannot be underestimated. As a superpower whose influence is felt all over the world, the United States can claim a "special" relationship with almost every other nation. Yet many Americans know very little about the histories of the nations with which the United States relates. How did they get to be the way they are? What kind of political systems have evolved there? What kind of influence do they have in their own region? What are the dominant political, religious, and cultural forces that move their leaders? These and many other questions are answered in the volumes of this series.

The authors who have contributed to this series have written comprehensive histories of their nations, dating back to prehistoric times in some cases. Each of them, however, has devoted a significant portion of the book to events of the last thirty years, because the modern era has contributed the most to contemporary issues that have an impact on U.S. policy. Authors have made an effort to be as up-to-date as possible so that readers can benefit from the most recent scholarship and a narrative that includes very recent events.

In addition to the historical narrative, each volume in this series contains an introductory overview of the country's geography, political institutions, economic structure, and cultural attributes. This is designed to give readers a picture of the nation as it exists in the contemporary world. Each volume also contains additional chapters that add interesting and useful detail to the historical narrative. One chapter is a thorough chronology of important historical events, making it easy for readers to follow the flow of a particular nation's history. Another chapter features biographical sketches of the nation's most important figures in order to humanize some of the individuals who have contributed to the historical development of their nation. Each volume also contains a comprehensive bibliography so that those readers whose interest has been sparked may find out more about the nation and its history. Finally, there is a carefully prepared topic and person index.

Readers of these volumes will find them fascinating to read and useful in understanding the contemporary world and the nations that comprise it. As series editors, it is our hope that this series will contribute to a heightened sense of global understanding as we embark on a new century.

Frank W. Thackeray and John E. Findling
Indiana University Southeast

Acknowledgments

I am extremely grateful to a multitude of people without whom this book would not have been possible. I am indebted to many scholars who have written extensively about Panama, in particular, Michael Conniff of San José State University and Margaret Scranton of the University of Oklahoma. I would like to thank a number of colleagues who have supported me and my work in a variety of ways: Edward DeClair and Daniel Lang of Lynchburg College, Cliff Staten of Indiana University Southeast, and Frank Mora of the National Defense University. Extra special thanks go to former Panamanian presidents Ernesto Pérez Balladares and Arístides Royo for providing insightful interviews. I am appreciative of Steven Vetrano at Greenwood for making the writing process such a pleasure.

Heartfelt thanks go to my wife, Dora, for her patience during my long absences while writing and to my son, Trevor, who patiently waited for his dad to come out and play.

Dedicated to the indelible memory of Alexander H. McIntire Jr., whose profound intellectual influence affects me still.

Timeline of Historical Events

1501   Rodrigo Galván de las Bastides sights the San Blas Islands off Panama's coast.

1502   Christopher Columbus lands in Panama and leaves his brother Bartolomé to found the first Spanish settlement, which is destroyed by local Indians.

1510   The first royal government seat in the Americas, Santa María de La Antigua del Darién, is founded in Panama.

1513   Vasco Núñez de Balboa leads an expedition west across Panama and becomes the first European to see the Pacific Ocean from the Americas.

1567   Panama is incorporated into the Viceroyalty of Peru.

1572   English pirate Francis Drake temporarily captures the port of Nombre de Dios.

1671   Henry Morgan invades Panama with a fleet of 35 ships and over 2,000 English and French privateers, and sacks and destroys Panama City.

1739   A British fleet destroys the port of Puerto Bello.

1740   Panama is incorporated into the Viceroyalty of Nueva Granada.

1821   After first supporting the Spanish Crown against Latin American independence, Panama declares its independence, but then decides to join the Republic of Gran Colombia as a province.

1840   Panama exercises brief independence from Colombia during a civil war.

1846   The United States obtains permission from Colombia to build a railroad across Panama.

1848   The Bidlack-Mallarino Treaty is signed between Colombia and the United States, which gives the United States the right to intervene militarily in Panama.

1855   The Panama Railroad is completed

1856   The "Watermelon War" erupts between the United States and Panamanian citizens, resulting in the first U.S. military intervention in Panama.

1878   The French *Compagnie Universelle du Canal Interoceanique* is granted rights by Colombia to build a canal across Panama. Construction begins the next year under the direction of Ferdinand de Lesseps, builder of the Suez Canal.

1889   The French company declares bankruptcy after completing about 40 percent of the canal. Civil war erupts in Colombia, spreading to the Panamanian province in 1900.

1903   With U.S. military support, Panama declares its independence from Colombia. Panama signs the Panama Canal Treaty with the United States, which allows the United States to complete the canal.

1904   With U.S. support, President Amador disbands the Panamanian military. U.S. troops surround the presidential palace to protect Amador. Panama's first constitution is created. The U.S. dollar is made legal tender in Panama, and the Panama Canal Zone is created.

1905   Following the research of a Cuban doctor, U.S. army surgeon William Gorgas eradicates malaria in the Panama Canal Zone.

1913   Construction of the Panama Canal is completed.

1914   The Panama Canal is officially opened for business. The United States begins a military buildup in the Canal Zone, eventually reaching 14 military bases. The first American banks open in Panama City.

1931   With the support of the National Police, the *Acción Comunal* group overthrows the government of Florencio Harmodio Arosemena.

1941   President Arnulfo Arias is overthrown by the National Police, ostensibly for his profascist rhetoric. His successor, Ricardo Adolfo de la Guardia, declares war on the Axis powers after Pearl Harbor.

1958   A group of Panamanian students enters the Canal Zone to set up Panamanian flags, which results in a confrontation with U.S. and Panamanian troops in which 120 students die.

1959   Panamanian students again enter the Canal Zone to plant Panamanian flags and again are repelled by U.S. and Panamanian forces. The embassy of the United States is damaged.

1960   Roberto Chiari is elected president and becomes the first opposition candidate ever elected to the presidency.

1963   Under the Alliance for Progress, the School of the Americas is opened in the Canal Zone.

1964   Panamanian students enter the Canal Zone to fly Panama's flag at Balboa High School. U.S. students resist, and a three-day riot breaks out. This incident is the catalyst to a change in the canal treaty.

1967   U.S. President Johnson presents Panamanian President Robles with a draft of a new canal treaty. Noriega begins a 20-year relationship as a CIA informant.

1968   Arnulfo Arias is elected to a third term. Eleven days later he is overthrown again by the National Guard.

1969   Colonel Boris Martínez becomes head of the ruling junta but is soon replaced by Lieutenant Colonel (later General) Omar Torrijos.

1970   A new law allows for "off-shore" banking and secret accounts, making Panama one of the world's banking meccas.

1971   Father Héctor Gallego, a Colombian priest working in Panama, is arrested and murdered by Noriega's intelligence service, the G-2.

1972   Torrijos forms a Constitutional Reform Commission and creates the National Assembly of Corregimientos. Torrijos assumes title of "Maximum Leader of the Panamanian Revolution." Panama accuses the United States at the United Nations of colonization.

1973   Panama hosts the United National Security Council meeting at which Torrijos threatens "violent change" if the United States does not relent on the Panama Canal.

1977   Jimmy Carter and Omar Torrijos sign the Panama Canal Treaties, which will cede the canal to Panama at the end of 1999.

1978   The U.S. Senate approves the Canal Treaties. The Partido Democrático Revolucionaro is created and Law #81 legalizes the political opposition. Arístides Royo is appointed as a figurehead president.

1981   Omar Torrijos dies in a plane crash in western Panama.

1982   Arístides Royo is ousted by the National Guard, whose commander, Rubén Paredes, assumes control of the country.

1983   A national referendum is held on constitutional reforms. Noriega becomes head of the National Guard and ousts Paredes. Noriega assumes the de facto leadership of the country.

1984   Nicolás Ardito Barletta, heading a six-party coalition ticket called the National Democratic Union, wins a rigged election and becomes Noriega's puppet president.

1985   Anti-Noriega activist Hugo Spadafora is brutally murdered by the G-2, setting off protests within Panama. President Ardito Barletta calls for an investigation and is pressured to resign by Noriega.

1987   Panama's per capita foreign debt becomes the highest in all of Latin America.

1988   Noriega is indicted for drug trafficking in Miami and Tampa. President Delvalle tries to fire Noriega but is fired himself. Panama's Chief of Police, Leonidas Macías, mounts an unsuccessful coup against Noriega.

1989   Noriega's progovernment coalition, COLINA, wins tainted elections and members of the opposition are beaten bloody on worldwide television. Moisés Giraldi attempts a nearly successful coup against Noriega but is killed. Under increasing pressure from the United States, Noriega declares that "a state of war exists" between the two countries. The United States invades Panama with 24,000 troops. Defeated presidential candidate Guillermos Endara is installed as president by U.S. forces

1990   Disgruntled former Panamanian military officers mount an attempted coup against Endara, which is put down by U.S. military forces.

1992   Panama's first nationwide vote since the invasion is held to consider amendments to the Torrijos-era constitution.

1994   A constitutional amendment is approved that disbands and prohibits a standing military. Ernesto Pérez Balladares, a candidate for the PRD, is elected as president.

1995   A Hong Kong–based Chinese company, Hutchinson Whampoa, wins a contract to run Panama's ports. Panamanian government names a new Canal Commission to oversee the canal's transition and informal talks begin on possible U.S. presence in Canal after 2000.

1997   Pérez Balladares proposes bill that would allow presidential re-election for the first time.

1998   Negotiations take place to discuss a limited U.S. military presence at certain military bases past the year 2000; the negotiations are unsuccessful. The Panamanian government accuses Gustavo Gorriti, a Peruvian journalist working for the Panamanian daily *La Prena*, of slandering the attorney general.

1999   Mireya Moscoso, the widow of Arnulfo Arias, becomes Panama's first female president. At 12 noon on December 31, the United States cedes control of the Panama Canal.

2002   Thirty-six grave sites of victims of the dictatorship are discovered on former military bases.

2003   Panama begins to militarize its border with Colombia after incursions by Colombian drug traffickers.

2004   Martín Torrijos, son of Omar, is elected president over former president Guillermo Endara. Panama is rated one of the three freest countries in Latin America.

1

Panama Is a Canal and More

The first thing that typically comes to mind when one thinks of Panama is the canal. This trans-isthmian waterway was a dream from the earliest days of Spanish colonization, but it was not realized until 1914 by the United States. This vital waterway allowed ships to shorten the transit time between the Atlantic and Pacific by over a month, and has become a crucial maritime trade link for many of the world's trading nations. But the canal is not just a convenient shortcut between two bodies of water; it is the thread that weaves together Panama's modern history. Panama's location occupying the narrowest section of the Central American isthmus not only made the canal possible, but has also defined the country's politics, society, and economy for more than five hundred years.

The importance of being at the geographical "crossroads of the world" has also made Panama the Latin American country most heavily influenced and shaped by the United States over the long term. The Panama Canal focused the economic and strategic interests of the United States more acutely and for much longer than any other place in the Western Hemisphere. Few other hemispheric issues elicited more heated debate than the long U.S. presence in the country or the eventual turnover of the canal. For this reason, modern Panamanian history can be appreciated

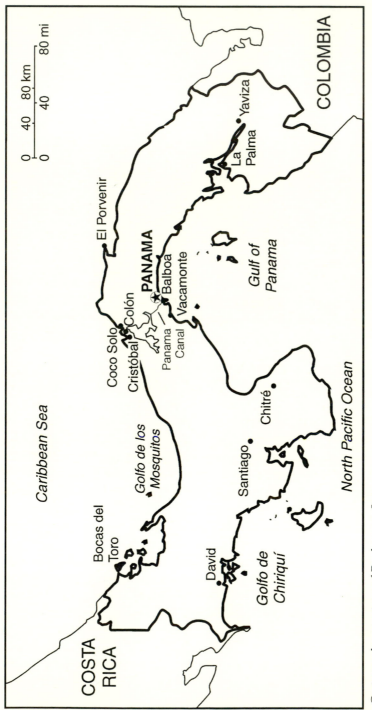

Cartography courtesy of Bookcomp, Inc.

only through a deep recognition of the intimate and lasting role of the United States in multiple aspects of Panamanian society.

First as a colony of Spain and after 1830 as a province of Colombia, Panama did not gain nominal independence until 1903 when, with U.S. military support, it seceded from Colombia and agreed under duress to permit the United States to finish the canal a French company had begun 25 years earlier. In response, U.S. President Theodore Roosevelt declared, ". . . I took the canal," and for almost one hundred years Panama existed as a protectorate of the United States, since the U.S. alone controlled the Canal Zone and therefore held considerable sway over the Panama's main source of income. Only after considerable struggle, perseverance, and even rioting and bloodshed did Panama convince the U.S. Congress to sign the Panama Canal treaties in 1978. These treaties stipulated Panama's assumption of full sovereignty over the waterway by the end of the millennium. However, the last leg of the road to full sovereignty was interrupted by the U.S. invasion of Panama in 1989, purportedly to put an end to dictator Manuel Noriega's drug trafficking. At least 3,000 Panamanian civilians died in the attack. True independence for Panama was finally achieved at the end of 1999 when the canal was handed over by the United States in a ceremony attended by former U.S. president Jimmy Carter, who had signed the treaties.

THE LAND AND ECONOMY

The isthmus of Panama occupies the narrowest section of Central America between Costa Rica to the northwest and Colombia to the southeast. Covering over 78,000 square kilometers, or almost the size of South Carolina, Panama is a warm, tropical country with only two seasons: hot, humid, and rainy from May to January and dry and hot from January to May. The land is bisected as well. The interior is characterized by rolling plains and a central spine of steep, rugged mountains, whose highest point is Volcán Barú at 3,454 meters. By contrast, the coastline is generally flat and possesses a number of natural harbors. Numerous islands dot the nearby ocean, including the Bocas del Toro archipelago near Costa Rica and the San Blas Islands in the Caribbean, a chain that extends for over 160 kilometers and is the home to one of the country's few remaining indigenous groups, the Kuna.

Located in the eastern part of the country is Darién, a province that covers almost one-third of the country. This area is a dense rainforest that has been recognized as one of the world's most ecologically diverse regions and declared a World Heritage Biosphere Reserve by UNESCO. The so-called "Darién Gap," the 87-kilometer-long missing section of the Pan-American Highway, begins near the town of Yaviza.

The Panama Canal area is a unique, though man-made, geographic region. Formerly called the "Panama Canal Zone," it is a 16-kilometer-wide area that bisects the isthmus, running 80 kilometers roughly north-south between the capital, Panama City, on the Pacific and the port of Colón on the Caribbean. The canal is the centerpiece of an immense watershed, covering 552,761 hectares. To provide water to the canal, the Chagres River was dammed to create Gatún Lake, which was, when created, the world's largest artificial lake. The rainfall produced by this tropical fresh-water watershed provides the only means for refilling the canal. For each passage, which takes about nine hours, a single vessel using the canal requires 197 million liters of fresh water. This means that with an average of 36 ships crossing daily, almost 7.6 billion liters of water are expended every day. The canal also provides 95 percent of the drinking water for the surrounding residents.

The Panama Canal is an engineering marvel in many other ways. Unlike the sea-level Suez canal in Egypt, which is essentially a very large ditch cut across the desert, the Panama Canal presented monumental engineering feats: cutting through mountains, building a railroad through jungle, and constructing two (later three) massive sets of concrete locks to raise and lower ships.

The corridor around the canal is significantly more developed than the rest of the country, and Panama City is home to almost every center of importance: financial, educational, social, cultural, and political. An important distinction is that the canal's presence has meant that Panama has had a very different modern economy than other Central American countries. While the rest of Central America's economies traditionally have depended almost exclusively on agricultural exports such coffee and bananas, the bulk of Panama's economy has been built around the canal. While Panama does export relatively small amounts of agricultural goods, its principle revenue comes from trade and financial services associated with the products that transit the waterway and from its banking sector.

The canal's tolls provide about 10 percent of the country's annual revenue. Every month, over 1,000 ships transit the canal, carrying 195 million metric tons and representing at least one-quarter of the world's sea trade. Though the canal's strategic and economic importance to the United States has decreased over the past decades, the United States is still the dominant country of origin and destination for products transiting the canal. The canal is also a vital conduit for many of the world's trading nations, particularly South American countries, which are proportionately much more dependent on the canal for their trade, and China, whose growing trade with Europe is tied to the canal. All vessels traversing the canal are charged tolls according to weight, averaging around $28,000.

But it is the canal-associated services that are more important to the economy, producing over 60 percent of Panama's gross domestic product. Banking and trade are the most significant activities, and their stability has been aided by the fact that Panama uses the U.S. dollar as its currency. Over 120 national and international banks dot Panama City's skyline with gleaming glass skyscrapers, making it the Western Hemisphere's second-largest international banking center (behind New York City), whose ultra-secret banking rules have traditionally provided lucrative "off-shore" financial services. Two other important enterprises directly related to the canal-driven economy are the Free Trade Zone in Colón, the world's second-largest such zone after Hong Kong, and the registration of foreign merchant ships under the Panamanian flag, which puts them under so-called "flags of convenience." Almost 5,000 of these ships are registered in Panama due to the country's lenient tax laws, making Panama the titular home to one of the largest merchant fleets in the world.

THE PEOPLE AND CULTURE

Panama's most well known musician, actor, and one-time presidential candidate, Rubén Blades, embodies many of the country's cultural characteristics. With English, American, Spanish, and Colombian grandparents, Blades's background as well as his music exhibit diversity: smooth salsa interwoven with Afro-Caribbean percussion and elements of jazz, rock, and blues. Blades exemplifies the complexities Panamanian society in general displays.

At its heart, Panamanian culture and traditional societal structures are rooted in the European and Hispanic traditions inherited from the original Spanish settlers. Some Hispanic traditions hold fast, such the *quinceñera*, a girl's fifteenth-birthday celebration, similar to a "sweet sixteen" party in the United States, but immensely more elaborate and formal. The extended family tends to be the center of a Panamanian's world, and social mobility opportunities are more frequently tempered by considerations of family proximity than is the case in the United States. But, while Panamanians continue to emphasize traditional relationships, they have become more accustomed to, if not inculcated with, North American sensibilities of time, exactitude, and business practices. This melding of attitudes leads to Panamanians being by and large more relaxed, easygoing, and informal than is common elsewhere in Latin America.

Nevertheless, Panamanians do maintain a regard for formal dignity as well as entrenched social views such as hierarchy, class distinctions, and machismo.

One of the most enduring debates is whether Panama's culture is more Central American or Caribbean. Though the cultural underpinnings are solidly Spanish-European, particularly for the upper class, the average Panamanian's cultural influences are considerably more Caribbean and African-influenced than is found in other Central American countries. For example, Afro-Caribbean rhythms punctuate some styles of Panamanian music that would not be out of place in Barbados or St. Lucia, and the lively, extravagant Lenten celebrations in Panama City could be easily mistaken for those of Brazil's famous *Carnival*.

With just over three million people, Panama has the smallest population among the countries of Spanish-speaking Latin America, but conversely, its population is more ethnically complex than most other countries in the region. Like its national dish *sancocho*, Panama's ethnic blend is complementary: All of the different ingredients retain their own distinct identity while adding flavor to the dish. While 70 percent of Panamanians are classified as mestizos, a mixture of European and Indian ancestry, there are substantial minorities of other groups, and almost every nuance of skin color and race is represented. About 10 percent of Panamanians are white, and they make up a very small, elite class that has traditionally been the most influential of Panama's political and economic decision makers. Many blacks, who make up another 10 percent, are descended either from escaped slaves (*cimarrones*) or West Indians who immigrated to build the trans-isthmus railroad in the mid-1800s and later, the canal. In addition, between the start of the failed French effort in 1881 to the canal's completion in 1914, an estimated 83,000 foreign workers entered Panama, making Chinese seamstresses, Arab traders, Korean shop owners, and English tailors all very common sites.

The last group is the indigenous people, who make up about 6 percent of the population. As in many Latin American countries, most Indians in Panama were killed by Spanish weapons, succumbed to European diseases, or were assimilated through intermarriage with Spaniards. Nonetheless, there are still small pockets of indigenous tribes that live much like their ancestors, mostly apart from modern Panamanian society and preserving traditional lifestyles and largely eschewing modernity. The most well known tribe is the Kuna, who live mainly in the San Blas Islands, a self-governed, semi-autonomous region. The Kuna have proudly preserved their culture and are perhaps best known for their unique, colorful textiles called *molas*, a multilayered, hand-stitched appliqué. However, the encroachment of modern society and financial exigency has forced an increasing number of young indigenous people to move to large cities to seek employment.

Most Panamanians live in and around the central region of the country dominated by the Panama Canal, principally in the Panama City metropolitan area but also in the large cities of Colón, Chitré, and David. By contrast, the densely forested Darién province and the mountainous northwest are sparsely populated.

Spanish is Panama's official language, and its speech is quite distinctive among Spanish-speaking countries for its rapidity and distinctive accent, laced with colloquialisms unique to Panama. Because of the long U.S. presence, English is a widely spoken second language in cities, particularly among the educated professional class. The relative wealth stemming from the canal and the long relationship with the United States have provided a relatively high standard of living. Education, health, and public works all register favorably in comparison to most other countries in the region. Today, after decades of public work begun during the Torrijos regime, almost 94 percent of Panamanians are literate. However, this progress is largely confined to the central region of the country around the canal. Thirty-seven percent of Panamanians live in poverty, and over half of these live in abject poverty. At least 20 percent of Panamanians still lack electricity or running water.[1]

Panama's constitution recognizes Roman Catholicism as the dominant, but not official, religion, but freedom of worship is protected. Nonetheless, 85 percent of Panamanians are nominal Catholics, and elements of the Catholic faith implicitly affect many aspects of everyday life: Holy days and saints' days are abundant on the Panamanian calendar; marriages traditionally involve separate civil and religious ceremonies; and children's life stages are marked by baptism, first communion, and confirmation. In contrast, many blacks continue to practice Protestantism, and there are also pockets of other faiths that practice freely, including Islam, Judaism, and Hinduism.

POLITICS AND RELATIONS WITH THE UNITED STATES

After the United States helped Panama to declare its independence from Colombia in 1903, President Theodore Roosevelt publicly declared that he "took the canal." For almost the next 100 years, the security of the Panama Canal would figure prominently in the U.S. expansion as a continental and commercial world power, and would be a primary catalyst for the reversal of historical U.S. isolationism. As Ambler Moss, Jr., former U.S. ambassador to Panama (1978–1982), stated, "U.S. interest in Panama [was], in descending order, the canal, U.S. military bases, and democracy." Thus, relations between the United States and Panama were based on the security and continued functioning of the canal, which meant that Panama's ability to govern itself was influenced and frequently hampered by the over-whelming U.S. presence. Noted historian of Latin America Michael Conniff has aptly encapsulated the nature of the resulting relationship as a "forced alliance."[2]

The Canal Zone was established as a de facto colonial outpost of the United States, governed by a treaty that stipulated that the United States could act "as if it were sovereign" within the Canal Zone, granting the U.S. "in perpetuity" control over all aspects of the canal. Until 1936, when the treaty was first revised, the isthmus existed in a legal-political limbo as a protectorate of the United States. Even crossing the Bridge of the Americas that spans the canal was a difficult passage for most Panaman-ians. In the Canal Zone, generations of U.S. citizens lived and worked in a miniature version of the United States: Bowling alleys, manicured lawns, Little League fields, and golf courses were all within sight, but out of reach of Panamanians. But in as much as they resented the division of their country, Panamanian politicians recognized, if grudgingly, the immense social and economic benefits the United States presence brought. The U.S. dollar became, and still is, Panama's currency, giving the country enviable monetary stability in Latin America. Health and education standards and practices introduced during the canal's construction became the corner-stone of Panama's social welfare system. For example, the structure of high school in Panama is much more similar to what is found in the United States than to that in any other Latin American country. This tension be-tween the nationalistic drive for autonomy contrasted with benefit seeking vis-à-vis the United States is a constant that defined Panamanian politics in the twentieth century.

Political actors in Panama have come from all corners of society, but modern politics in Panama has alternated principally between populist elite leaders and periods of military influence and rule. The oldest elite families, called the *rabiblancos* ("white-tails"), typically have lineages that can be traced to Spanish colonial times and have proportionally greater control over the country's wealth and power than is common in most other Latin American countries, except for perhaps El Salvador and its famous "14 families." Though the growth of professional political parties, labor movements, and over two decades of military rule have diminished the elites' ability to directly control politics, the majority of the country's presidents and government officials have come from this elite, with a handful of family names recurring often.

Until its abolition by constitutional amendment in 1994, the military in Panama frequently had a vested interest in influencing politics. But it was not until 1968 that the National Guard finally assumed direct control of the government in a coup d'état. General Omar Torrijos, an enigmatic yet pragmatic figure who led the country from 1968 to 1981, almost single-handedly revamped the country's political and social landscape through a combination of social reforms and was chiefly responsible for the Panama Canal treaties of 1978. On the other hand, his successor, Manuel Noriega, came to symbolize unfettered greed, duplicity, and cruelty until he was toppled by the U.S. invasion in December 1989.

Another important political group has been university students. Latin American universities traditionally have been hotbeds of political activism, but Panamanian students have been especially noteworthy in their ability to influence foreign policymaking. The largest student organization, the Federation of Panamanian Students (Federación de Estudiantes Panameños), led protest movements that were instrumental in starting the negotiations that led to the signing of the Panama Canal treaties.

Panama's modern political system is the direct result of its long relationship with the United States. It has a constitutional representative democracy with a government based on the U.S. model of three branches: executive, legislative, and judicial. The executive branch includes a president and two vice presidents. The president is elected by a direct, secret vote for a term of five years and may not seek consecutive reelection, but can run again after waiting for one term (as former President Guillermo Endara [1989–1994] did in the 2004 election). The president is both chief of state and head of government.

The legislative branch consists of a 78-member unicameral Legislative Assembly (Asamblea Legislativa), which contains representatives from nine provinces and one semi-autonomous territory (San Blas). Like the president, legislators are elected by popular vote to five-year terms, but the selection method differs depending on whether the representative comes from a rural or urban area: Legislators from rural districts are elected on a plurality basis whereas urban districts elect several legislators through a proportionally based formula.

The judicial branch is organized under a nine-member Supreme Court (Corte Suprema de Justicia) and includes all tribunals and municipal courts. Supreme Court justices are appointed for terms of 10 years. In addition, an autonomous Electoral Tribunal supervises all facets of elections, including voter registration, the election process, and the activities of political parties. Suffrage is compulsory for everyone 18 years of age and older, but non-voters are rarely, if ever, penalized. The legal system is based on French law but has received strong U.S. influence.

Panama has a multitude of political parties that rise and fall in accordance with election cycles, but two parties have become cornerstones of the political system. The left-leaning Partido Revolucionario Democrático (Democratic Revolutionary Party, or PRD) was founded in 1978 during the military dictatorship and originally cultivated strong ties to labor and the poor. The PRD was greatly influenced and partly modeled after Mexico's Institutional Revolutionary Party (PRI) due the latter's success at institutionalizing one-party rule.[3] During his regime, General Torrijos also sought to use the PRD as way to legitimize the military's rule. After his death in a plane crash in 1981 and Noriega's ouster in the 1989 U.S. invasion, the PRD captured the presidency with Ernesto Pérez Balladares in 1994. But in recent years the PRD has been unable to gather sufficient support to run candidates on its own and has needed coalitions with minor parties. This was the case in the 2004 victory of Martín Torrijos, son of Omar Torrijos, which required a coalition with several minor parties including the Partido Popular (People's Party). The Partido Arnulfista (Arnulfista Party) is named after three-time president Arnulfo Arias, who all three times was ousted by military coups. A right-of-center coalition of nationalists, it also has increasingly formed alliances with less-traditional minor parties.

Panamanians entered the new millennium full of hope and apprehension. On December 31, 1999, Panama assumed full control of the canal as well as all the lands and facilities that existed in the former Canal Zone. Though the United States maintains token interest in Panama, mainly in the form of anti-drug-trafficking assistance, Panama is now completely sovereign and entirely responsible for its future. But for almost a century, the history of Panama was intricately interwoven with the foreign policy concerns of the United States in the Western Hemisphere.

NOTES

1. World Bank, Panama Country Report, (www.worldbank.org), 2004.

2. Michael L. Conniff, *Panama and the United States: The Forced Alliance* (Athens: University of Georgia Press, 1992), 2.

3. Robert C. Harding II, *Military Foundations of Panamanian Politics* (New Brunswick, NJ: Transaction Publishers, 2001), 140–147.

2

Colonial Panama to Independence

Since rising out of the ocean four million years ago to become the bridge between North and South America, the isthmus of Panama has been a link of culture, trade, and travel for the hemisphere, and later, the world. This relationship is a primary recurring theme throughout its history. According to the most recent evidence, as early as 12,000 B.C.E. humans lived in Panama and used the isthmus as a transit point into South America. Even thousands of years ago, these original Panamanians used their central location for trade, occasionally with the Aztecs and Incas. Today's Kuna, Ngöbe, Buglere, and Guaymí tribes are descendents of these original people. When the Spanish explorers arrived, they found the area to be densely populated by an estimated 700,000 to 1,000,000 Amerindians. These societies were highly organized theocracies led by a chieftain, called a *cacique*, who stood atop a social hierarchy that included soldiers, priests, commoners, and slaves. The coming of Europeans only expanded the nature of the isthmus's importance, and from the beginning the strategic position of the isthmus determined its future.

ESTABLISHING THE COLONY

Spanish exploration and settlement of Panama began at the beginning of the sixteenth century. After his first voyage in 1492, Christopher

Columbus's reports of the New World set off a flurry of exploration of the Americas. In 1501 a wealthy Spaniard, Rodrigo Galván de las Bastides, who had accompanied Columbus on his second voyage to the Americas (1493–1496), was the first European to sight the San Blas Islands while sailing off Panama's north coast. However, his rotting ships forced him to return to Spain without exploring the interior. It would be Columbus, on his fourth and final voyage to the New World, who would explore Panama's Caribbean coast in 1502.

After local Indians showed him bits of gold, Columbus left to seek its source, leaving his brother, Bartolomé, and 80 men to found the first Spanish settlement in Panama, called Santa María de Belén. The Spaniards soon captured the local Indian *cacique*, resulting in war with his tribe. The resulting conflict destroyed the Spanish settlement and forced the survivors to temporarily abandon Panama.

Back in Spain, Columbus reported that the native people of Panama had gold in abundance, even using it as fishing weights. This description fit aptly into one of the three driving motivations for Spanish exploration and colonization of the New World: gold, God, and glory. In a wave of religious fanaticism and newfound political unity following the final defeat in 1492 of the invading Moors, Spain had turned fervently to the New World in the pursuit of gold, religious conversion, and new lands. Panama's worth to the Spanish Crown in all three areas had been established.

The Spanish monarchs, Fernando and Isabel, ordered the immediate resettlement of Panama. After several forays along Panama's Caribbean coast, the Spanish settlement of Santa María de La Antigua del Darién was established in 1510, becoming the first *cabildo* (royal government seat) in the Americas. The settlement's mayor, Vasco Núñez de Balboa, who had originally been a member of Bastides's crew, heard from the Indians that gold was plentiful in the "South Sea." Balboa, accompanied by 190 soldiers and a pack of dogs, headed south, hacking through the thick jungle.[1] Twenty-eight days later they became the first Europeans to see the Pacific Ocean from the Americas. Dressed in a full suit of armor, Balboa waded into the ocean and claimed it and all land bordering it for Spain.

By the mid-1500s, Panama's economic fortunes were bright. In 1538, the administration of all Spain's colonies from Nicaragua to Cape Horn was based in Panama in a royal court called an *audiencia*, but the court was soon reduced to governing just the isthmus. After 1567 Panama was incorporated into the Viceroyalty of Peru but retained its own *audiencia*. In the early sixteenth century, Nombre de Dios in Panama was one of only three ports (along with Veracruz in Mexico and Cartagena in Colombia) authorized by the Spanish crown for trade with the motherland, especially in precious metals. By royal decree, one-fifth (*quinto real*) of all New World gold and silver were bound for Spain's royal coffers, which Spain then used to fund its ongoing wars in Europe. This made Panama the focal point for Spain's search for wealth in the New World. Spain's gold and silver income grew by over 3,500 percent during the sixteenth century, much of it flowing through Panama. Upwards of 200,000 tons of silver and probably more gold crossed Panama during this time.

In addition, Panama's Pacific coast became the springboard for the invasion and conquest of the Incan Empire in Peru led by Francisco Pizarro. The vast wealth generated by these incursions was carried overland in Panama along the Camino Real (Royal Road) from the Pacific port of Panama City overland to Porto Bello on the Caribbean so that it could be loaded onto caravels bound for Spain. Panama quickly became the crossroads and marketplace for Spain in the New World. For the next 200 years, the bulk of the pilfered gold, as well as other American products like tobacco, crossed Panama en route to Spain, and manufactured goods from Europe poured in for the colonists, creating a symbiotic trading relationship that became known as the "Columbian Exchange."

In Panama, like elsewhere in Latin America, the Spanish enslaved the indigenous people to work the mines and fields. Within a couple of generations most indigenous peoples had either succumbed to Spanish swords or, more often, to common European diseases to which the Indians had no immunity. The decimation of the Indians, along with the Spanish distaste for hard labor, guaranteed the growth of the African slave trade in the mid-1500s. Panama was a principal distribution point for slaves bound for other parts of Spanish America.[2] Blacks quickly became infused into the colony's ethnic composition. By 1610, a census of Panama City showed that three-fourths of the population was black or mulatto. Since early Spanish explorers and settlers rarely brought wives from Europe, Panama's ethnic potpourri soon became the established norm. However, it was whites who remained atop the economic and political hierarchy.

By 1670, Panama City was the wealthiest city in the New World, and the overflowing chests of gold passing through Panama did not go unnoticed. Spain's main rivals in Europe, England and France, were eager to break Spain's monopoly on New World riches any way they could. These contenders actively sought to establish their own colonies in the region to counter Spain's growing power. In 1655 English warships forced Spain to surrender Jamaica and began to threaten the Spanish colony of Cuba as well as Spanish trade transiting the Caribbean from Panama. But the most direct threat to Panama's gold trade was the burgeoning pirate fleets that prowled the waters off Panama, making the isthmus their prime target. Piracy would have a lasting impact on the nascent colony.

Many of the most well known pirates earned at least part of their infamy attacking laden ships leaving Panama or the Panamanian mainland itself, sometimes with the support of Spain's enemies. For example, England's Francis Drake, with the covert support of Queen Elizabeth, briefly captured the Panamanian port of Nombre de Dios in 1572. Over the next 20 years Drake repeatedly raided Spanish galleons and pillaged Panamanian ports, eventually being knighted by the English queen for his service. Spanish buccaneers reciprocated, attacking Jamaica and other English as well as French colonies throughout the Caribbean. Though England and Spain concluded an agreement in 1670 to end hostilities, Henry Morgan invaded Panama the following year with a fleet of 35 ships and over 2,000 English and French privateers. He defeated the large Spanish force defending Panama City and sacked and burned the capital to the ground. A new capital was constructed on a more defensible site eight kilometers away, which today is the site of modern Panama City.

Just as Panama's location had been the cause of its boon times, it then became the cause of its decline. By the beginning of the 1700s South America's gold and silver mines were beginning to be exhausted, and Panama's privileged trading position waned accordingly. Other factors also contributed to the decline. The new Bourbon Spanish Crown had authorized more ports in Spanish America for trade, and continued high tariffs further decreased Panama's trade. To counter both these obstacles Panamanians engaged in ever bolder acts of smuggling and black marketeering. A final ironic blow to Panama's economic health was that the gold wealth that had attracted the pirates had made the Caribbean so hazardous that Spanish ships began to opt for the longer but safer route around South America from Peru's gold mines.

The coup de grâce occurred in 1739 when a British fleet destroyed the port of Porto Bello and Spain finally removed Panama's trading privileges. Panama's autonomy was withdrawn, and from 1740 to 1821 the isthmus became a forgotten backwater area as part of the Viceroyalty of Nueva Granada, which included present-day Colombia, Venezuela, Peru, and Ecuador. During this period, the diffusion of trade around Spanish America, more relaxed trade rules, and a significant reduction in the frequency of trade fleets to Panama meant that Panamanians were left largely to fend for themselves. Panama's economic foundation was not sufficiently diversified to take advantage of the liberalization, since Spain still discouraged the domestic production of finished goods in the Americas. To survive, Panamanian merchants became increasingly involved in contraband, particularly with British merchants in Jamaica. Panama's fortunes were sinking along with the weakening Spanish empire. This shared misery helped to foster a growing sense of national identity on the isthmus.

FLEETING INDEPENDENCE

While Panama's strategic position determined its economics, its geography also became the key to its political future. The first solid proposal for a canal through Panama was offered by the French to the Spanish government in 1786. Offers by budding South America revolutionaries to extend canal concessions through Panama to Britain and the United States became part of the early maneuvers toward Spanish-American independence. In fact, in 1787, future revolutionary leader Francisco Miranda of Venezuela "invited" Britain to invade the isthmus in exchange for financial assistance for the imminent revolution against Spain. The United States had also shown interest in such a canal. Thomas Jefferson had envisioned a canal across the isthmus as an economic tool for the country, but the young U.S. isolationist policies and westward growth excluded any type of concrete action in Panama. War with Spain put further canal plans on hold.

The beginning of the nineteenth century saw Spanish America simmering with resentment against Spain. Antagonism and bitterness grew between *criollos*, those of Spanish descent who were born in the Americas, and *peninsulares* (Spaniards born in Spain). *Peninsulares* were normally appointed to the most important government positions, while native-born *criollos* were systematically overlooked. Combined with Spain's continued restrictions on Panama trading with other nations, a volatile situation had been created in Spanish America that only needed a spark to ignite.

That spark came in 1807 when Napoléon's army invaded the Iberian Peninsula and deposed the Spanish monarchy. Realizing the golden opportunity presented by the motherland's upheaval, Latin American leaders made their move for independence. The struggle for Spanish American independence took many forms. In Mexico and South America the war against Spanish rule was long and bloody. It produced heroic figures like the "Liberator" Simón Bolívar, who is considered by many to be South America's "George Washington," and Argentina's venerated José de San Martín, whose army's treacherous march across the Andes Mountains to engage Spanish forces has become legendary, and has even been compared to Hannibal's crossing of the Alps.

But while most of Spanish America was engulfed in revolution, Panama remained a royal outpost, even sending soldiers to fight against the revolutionaries. When Nueva Granada's Spanish viceroy was deposed by the growing revolutionary tide, he moved the royal post to Panama. However, the war's deleterious effects on trade, the viceroy's death in 1821, and the subsequent military government's abuse of its once-loyal subjects resulted in Panamanians finally declaring their independence from Spain on November 28 of the same year with little fanfare or bloodshed. Panama's loyalty to the crown, it turned out, was second to its access to free trade and the budding *panameñismo* (the sense of being Panamanian). After spirited discussion among Panama's mercantile elites and large landowners in a *cabildo abierto* (open town meeting), the decision was made to join Bolívar's Republic of Gran Colombia, the post-independence successor to the colonial Nueva Granada.

From the outset of independence, Panama found itself in the middle of power plays between larger powers. Britain and the United States almost immediately began negotiating with Gran Colombia for trading rights, and Panama's economic policy was being determined in Bogotá, frustrations that stoked even more nationalistic sentiment on the isthmus. Panama's sense of self-importance was inflated by Simón Bolívar, who declared in 1822 in a letter to fellow revolutionary José de Fabrega, "I cannot express the joy and admiration I've felt knowing that Panama, the center of the Universe, is free by its own will." To substantiate this importance, Bolívar chose to convene a congress in Panama City in 1826 for Mexico, Central America, Colombia, and Peru. Here, in his "center of the universe," Bolívar tried to unify the region under one government. But local and regional disputes and power grabbing meant that the treaty was ultimately ratified only by Colombia, and the federation fell apart after Bolívar's death in 1830. After Gran Colombia's breakup, Panama remained a province of the new country, Nueva Granada (later renamed Colombia).

Despite Panama's being a Colombian province, its leaders were very eager to cultivate nationalist feelings. Panama's first official postindependence act was to liberalize trade rules to try to rekindle economic growth. But for the next two decades the Panamanian province languished in relative isolation, largely ignored by the government in Bogotá. Several minor, ill-fated attempts at Panamanian independence were thwarted by the Colombian government between 1830 and 1840. The first was led by the acting governor of Panama, but reincorporated the province at the urging of Bolívar, who was on his deathbed. The second try for independence was concocted by a would-be dictator, who was quickly deposed and executed. The third attempt in 1840 was briefly successful, capitalizing on a civil war that had erupted in Colombia between the conservatives and liberals. Panama was peacefully reintegrated into Colombia the following year.

However, interest in a canal located somewhere in Central America continued to grow, and Panama's strategic position again put it in the crosshairs of hemispheric geopolitical struggles. The U.S. Monroe Doctrine of 1826 had declared the Western Hemisphere a U.S. sphere of influence and had warned European powers not to try to establish further colonies in Latin America. But this admonition was an empty threat, since the United States at the time had fewer cannons than Britain had warships, and the British knew it. Consequently, the first half of the nineteenth century saw the British government brazenly establishing footholds in Central America. In 1848 the British seized the Nicaraguan town of San Juan del Norte at the mouth of the San Juan River and renamed it Greytown. This outpost and others on the Caribbean coast were points from which to explore possible canal routes (one settlement eventually became British Honduras—modern-day Belize).

In addition, the British were actively probing the Colombian government for trade concessions and a possible canal route across Panama. When Britain indicated that it was about to make territorial claims on Bocas del Toro in Panama, perhaps by force, the U.S. government took advantage of the Colombian government's fears of British incursion to cut an advantageous and opportune deal. In 1846 the United States successfully negotiated a treaty with the administration of Colombia's president, Tomás Cipriano Mosquera, which gave the United States transit rights through Panama, for which the United States would guarantee Colombian sovereignty over Panama against all foreign incursions, particularly the British.

Ratified in the U.S. Congress in 1848, the Bidlack-Mallarino Treaty (named after the U.S. and Colombian representatives, respectively) gave the United States the right to intervene militarily in Panama to protect financial and human interests and marked an important turning point in Panamanian history as well as the first step in a tumultuous 150-year relationship between Panama and the United States. From this point on, Panama's domestic sovereignty would be tempered, and at times limited, by geopolitical policy goals of successive U.S. administrations. Equally important, the treaty marked the first major, ongoing overseas commitment for the United States.

Surprised at being outmaneuvered, British outrage at the upstart Americans came close to triggering war. The situation was diffused in 1850 by the Clayton-Bulwer Treaty, which stipulated Anglo-American cooperation in the building and use of any future canal in the region and prohibited the establishment of colonies or fortifications in Central America. It was a highly contentious agreement in the United States among U.S. Democrats, who thought that it betrayed the intent of the Monroe Doctrine since it gave tacit approval of the status quo ante. But the treaty was most useful in that it gave the United States breathing room to resolve its impending civil war and to expand its military power in the Caribbean basin, of which Panama was considered a vital part. But in the end, as historian Michael Conniff notes, " the United States mostly tried to ignore Clayton-Bulwer in its relations with Panama, rejecting occasional British protests."[3] The treaty was transformed over the succeeding fifty years into an empty promise, as the United States slowly but steadily increased its economic and political interests in the isthmus.

But the transcontinental growth of the United States, not the threat of war, ultimately proved to be the catalyst for reenergizing Panama's fortunes. The creation of the Oregon territory and the annexation of California in 1848 had produced the need in the United States for faster mail routes to the West Coast. The discovery of gold in California the following year created a virtual westward stampede of "Argonauts," as the gold seekers were called. Taking up to a year from the East Coast by wagon, the long and dangerous journey claimed up to 10 percent of travelers and required precise timing to avoid Rocky Mountain snows. By contrast, the fastest and safest alternative was by boat to Panama, where prospectors would cross the isthmus and, on the Pacific side, take a boat up the coast to the California goldfields. By comparison, this route took only five weeks to complete.

THE PANAMA RAILROAD

The Bidlack-Mallarino Treaty had granted the United States transit rights across Panama, and a railroad was the solution to the rapid movement of people, mail, and, once again, gold—this time from California. An American entrepreneur, William H. Aspinwall, and a group of New York investors were awarded a contract by the U.S. government in 1847 to provide faster mail service for the West Coast of the United States. To speed up the normal transit across the isthmus by mule, Aspinwall would build a railroad across Panama to link up the steamer routes coming from each coast.

The British also saw practical benefits to a faster link, which would provide a shorter trade route to its colonial possessions in Asia. They had conducted studies on the possibility of building a railroad or even a canal, but investor interest crumbled under the weight of the challenges to construction. For similar reasons, France wished to establish a railway and even went so far as entering into a contract in 1848 with Colombia (then called Nueva Granada). But, again, once the cost of surmounting the geography was completely understood, the company backed out and went bankrupt within a year. Up against seemingly impossible odds, Aspinwall and his investors were able to negotiate a lucrative construction contract with the new free-trade-friendly Colombian government in 1850, in which they received free land on which to build and operate the railroad for up to 49 years. Colombia had the option to purchase it from the company after 20 years. This first business negotiation on the isthmus involving Americans set the tone for future deals there.

The obstacles were considerable. In addition to swamps, mountains, incessant mosquitoes, and torrential tropical downpours, the builders faced labor shortages as well as diseases such as malaria and yellow fever that ravaged the workforce. Though Panamanians built an accompanying highway and served as guides and boatmen for the project, relatively few Panamanians showed interest in performing the grueling and dangerous work of laying the railroad. In response, Aspinwall imported labor from around the world. West Indians (mostly Jamaicans), Africans, Chinese, English, Irish, and Germans all came to build the railroad, and around the work zone these immigrants came to equal, if not outnumber, native Panamanians. According to accounts of the time, a large percentage of these immigrant workers began to fall ill from tropical diseases almost as soon as they arrived. Sickness, harsh working conditions, and anxiety took their toll. Suicide, particularly among the Chinese, was commonplace. Legend has it that every railroad tie laid across Panama corresponded to a fallen worker. The railroad's construction not only began to intertwine the economic interests of Panama and the United States, but also foreshadowed the geographic as well as social and political challenges that building the canal would pose.

The construction of the Panama Railroad, which began to diversify Panama's social makeup, was an important catalyst that also sparked dormant Panamanian nationalist sentiments. The Caribbean port that the railroad built had been christened "Aspinwall," after its owner, but Panamanians defiantly called it "Colón" instead, after the Spanish version of the surname of Christopher Columbus. Though some Americans stubbornly insisted on the English name, the Panamanian name eventually won out, partially due to Panamanians postal workers' refusal to recognize "Aspinwall" as a legitimate postal address.

The large volume of travelers through Panama naturally attracted unsavory characters of all types who took advantage of the lack of law enforcement. Panama became a Latin American "Wild West." Since Colombia provided relatively few police in its Panama province, Aspinwall contracted and brought in experienced U.S. law enforcement personnel to impose order and to safeguard the railway's construction.

A former Texas Ranger named Randolph Runnels was hired to form what became known as the "Isthmus Guard," which developed into Panama's first intelligence and law enforcement agency. Composed of Americans and supplemented by Mexicans, Chileans, and Peruvians, but no Panamanians, the Isthmus Guard used a variety of terror tactics to impose order. The most notorious incident occurred in 1852 when 37 suspected criminals suffered summary execution by the Guard, their bodies hung on a wall as a warning to would-be criminals. On at least one occasion, the guard also functioned as a strike-buster, dispelling Panamanian workers who tried to organize. Though the Guard was dissolved following the railroad's completion, its heavy-handed tactics and exclusion of local law enforcement officials began to predispose Panamanians toward suspicion of American motives and to build resistance to the American presence.

Completed in 1855 and costing over $7 million, the Panama Railroad was the most expensive railway built up to that time, requiring 170 bridges to cover the 80 kilometers from coast to coast. Though it cost more than the original $5 million estimate, its utility and profitability to its investors became apparent almost instantly. With a decade, its annual profits were over $11 million and it was transporting thousands of passengers daily. So profitable was the railroad that the company reconsidered its original business agreement with Colombia and renegotiated an agreement to essentially allowed Aspinwall's company to keep the railroad. Over 600,000 people crossed Panama from 1848 until the completion of the U.S. transcontinental railroad in 1869.

The completion of the Panama Railroad was a boon to its U.S. investors, despite the competition offered by a contemporary transit route across Nicaragua operated by Cornelius Vanderbilt. It also was valuable to Panama's economy, since cash flow grew exponentially and many wealthy foreign businessmen set up shop in Panama City. However, the benefits were far fewer for common Panamanians. Thousands of local workers were left unemployed, disgruntled, and angry both at the American company and at the growing American control of the entire zone surrounding the railroad. The American community had grown quickly and become a contending economic and cultural force. Panamanians were beginning to feel like foreigners in their own land. Americans also brought with them virulent racism common at the time in the United States, insensitivity toward Panamanian culture, and a sense of superiority that bordered on megalomania. The dollar and English displaced the peso and Spanish, and the first major newspaper to be published in Panama was the English-language *Panama Star and Herald*. Its publisher, Archibald Boyd, was an American immigrant to Panama, and his son, Federico Boyd, became one of the ten founders of independent Panama and briefly held the presidency in 1910.

THE WATERMELON WAR AND INTERVENTION

Panamanians' frustrations boiled over in the so-called "Watermelon War" in 1856. Among the droves of Americans crossing Panama were many unsavory types who, according to contemporary accounts, were little more than criminals. All too often, they passed their time drunk while waiting for ships and frequently showed their contempt for Panama's mixed races. One such traveler helped himself to the fruit from a poor black Panamanian vendor. When the American refused to pay and the vendor protested, the traveler produced a pistol, causing Panamanians to respond in kind. At least 16 people were killed in the ensuing melee, which was put down by Runnels's Isthmus Guard.

A report sent to Washington detailing the incident recommended a military occupation of the isthmus, based on the "colored population's hatred of Americans" and the Colombian government's "inability to maintain order." Coupled with derogatory newspaper reports of Panamanians' shiftlessness, including an uncomplimentary article printed in the *Chicago Republican* by a young Samuel Clemens, public opinion toward Panama in the United States was tilted toward military intervention. Six months later, U.S. soldiers landed in Panama City and briefly took control of the railroad station. The United States justified the intervention through the Monroe Doctrine and the Bidlack-Mallarino treaty with Colombia, in which the United States had pledged to keep Panama open to free transit. Adding insult to injury, Colombia was forced to pay $412,000 in restitution to the railroad for damages, further embittering public opinion in Panama toward the United States.

This was the first U.S. military intervention in Panama, but thirteen more would occur before Panama's independence from Colombia 47 years later. The Watermelon War underscored two themes that would recur during the next fifty years: the frequency with which the United States would use force to protect its economic interest in Panama and the way in which American cultural and racial beliefs of the time would be implanted in the isthmus. Despite British protests under the terms of the Clayton-Bulwer Treaty, Panama had become a protectorate of the United States. But the issue of sovereignty in the transit zone would define Panamanians' sense of nationalism, the country's economic system, and its geopolitical future. The railroad's utility as a vital link between the two U.S. coasts had become patently clear, and the strategic value of the isthmus became imbedded in the minds of U.S. policymakers, an idea that would endure for almost a century and a half.

THE CANAL'S FALSE START

Even as the Panama Railroad continued to move people and goods across the isthmus, the idea of a canal somewhere in Central America continued to percolate among would-be builders, and Colombia wanted it to be built in its neglected Departmento de Panamá. Soon after the end of the U.S. Civil War in 1865, negotiations for a canal began between Washington and Bogotá. Colombia had recently purchased the Panama Railroad and its accompanying land and was eager to capitalize on Panama's ripe location for a canal.

Though the venture was profitable, the inflexibility of the Panama Railroad's directors in pricing had eventually driven away many of its South American customers. The completion in 1869 of both the transcontinental railroad in the United States and the Suez Canal in Egypt had created a sense of expansionism that naturally seemed to include a canal somewhere in Central America. However, its location was far from decided. Both the British and Americans had been exploring the possibility of a route through Nicaragua, which would use a course down the San Juan River to Lake Nicaragua, leaving only a 20-kilometer canal to be cut through mountains lower than those in Panama. All things considered, it was a promising alternative to Panama, except that the San Juan River formed the part of the border between Nicaragua and Costa Rica, whose governments could not agree on the border's exact location within the river.

In 1870, the United States offered Colombia what amounted to joint ownership of the canal as well as military protection and a 10 percent share of the profits, increasing to 25 percent after the initial investment was paid off. British complaints that the offer violated the Clayton-Bulwer Treaty were deflected by the United States on the technicality that Panama was part of Colombia, a South American nation, and the treaty only covered activities in Central America. However, U.S. demands for transit priority in wartime, Secretary of State Seward's opposition to the canal's neutrality, and the relatively low profit margin ultimately gave the Colombian Senate sufficient reason to reject the offer. Undiscouraged, and to hedge its position, the United States began actively investigating Nicaragua as an alternative canal location. But Panama's potential was not ignored for long.

In 1878, a French company, the Compagnie Universelle du Canal Interoceanique (Universal Company of the Inter-Ocean Canal), was granted exclusive rights by Colombia to build a canal, which was to be completed within 12 years. In exchange, Colombia would receive 5 percent of the profits and $250,000 annually. The agreement stipulated that the canal was to be neutral and would revert to Colombia after 99 years. President Rutherford B. Hayes tried to warn off the French and even sent warships to loom off Panama's coast, but neither Colombia nor France was intimidated by the show of force and called Hayes's bluff.

Construction began in 1879 to much fanfare and prognostications of success. The project's director, Ferdinand de Lesseps, had established himself as the famed promoter and financier of the Suez Canal. Lesseps proposed a sea-level canal for Panama similar to the Suez, but many monumental challenges were yet to be resolved, particularly how to surmount the obstacle posed by Panama's 3,300-meter-tall mountains. One imaginative, but impractical, proposal called for a ship tunnel through the mountains. But, as was the case during the construction of the Panama Railroad, the French soon learned that the greatest challenge that confronted them was not geography but epidemiology. Yellow fever and malaria exacted an excruciatingly high toll on workers. Within two years of beginning construction, workers stricken with these illnesses were filling the French-run hospitals, such as l'Hôspital Nôtre Dame du Canal on the outskirts of Panama City. Between 50 and 75 percent of French officials who came to work in Panama died from disease, which explains why in France Panama was given the unflattering moniker of the "white man's graveyard."

The French recognized that sanitation in some way was at the root of the problem, but still did not understand disease transmission well enough to figure out the carrier. When the French arrived, the streets of Panama City and Colón were unpaved, garbage-filled, and reeked of putrefaction. To make matters worse, abject poverty was the rule, not the exception. Many residents, some of whom had been left unemployed by the railroad's completion, lived in squalid shacks and tenements on land that flooded frequently during the rainy season. These conditions fit perfectly into the French supposition of the day that decaying matter and dirty living conditions caused yellow fever.

But the workers continued coming. Though some came from neighboring Spanish-speaking countries, the majority was blacks, principally from Jamaica, but a significant minority escaping the post-Civil War United States. In addition to French engineers, American, German, Russian, and

Italian expertise was also utilized. The work zone effectively became a United Nations before its time. Between 1883 and 1887 an estimated 15,000 workers were on the job full time, but they continued to die at prodigious rates. One estimate put the toll at 200 workers per month. Some were stricken as soon as they arrived in Panama, such as in 1885 when the new French consul died within a week after arriving. The French company pressed on with the arduous task of blasting and excavating the land. The array of then state-of-the-art construction equipment was both impressive and ridiculous. For example, Americans pundits of the time derided the French for sending snow shovels to a place "where snow never has fallen."[4]

The difficulty of the dig and the toll of disease slowed work considerably, causing the company's stock value to fall accordingly. Even when it became obvious to others that a sea-level canal was not possible, Lesseps persisted, sure that his genius would overcome the difficulty. Facing serious debt, Lesseps finally relented, employing a soon-to-be famous Parisian builder named Eiffel to design locks for the canal. But it was a case of too little, too late. Lesseps faced obstacles on all fronts. Some hampered his attempt at emergency financing by spreading rumors of failure and dumping stocks and bonds on the market. Corrupt French politicians and bureaucrats demanded large bribes to approve the issue of further stock. Lastly, his effort to get the French government to guarantee his bonds was blocked by the United States, on the grounds that it would lead to French government control of the canal, which would violate the Monroe Doctrine. On February 4, 1889, Lesseps's company declared bankruptcy, taking with it the life savings of hundreds of thousands of French investors.

In the end, the French company had completed about 40 percent of the excavation necessary for the canal and had built a good number of buildings and hospitals that would eventually be used by the United States. The tragic endnote was that this accomplishment had cost at least 22,000 workers their lives, though the actual number is probably higher—since workers were charged a day's wages for care in company hospitals, many just chose to die elsewhere for free.

THE TURNING POINT

Panama might have lingered on for a few more decades with a partially completed canal, but geopolitical events again created a restructuring of power that affected the isthmus. The Spanish-American War of 1898 was an important turning point in the hegemonic tug-of-war that had been occurring in the Caribbean for centuries. On February 15, 1898 the U.S.

battleship *Maine* exploded in Havana harbor. Aided by corrupt yellow journalistic practices, the furor that erupted in the United States woke a sleeping giant out of its self-imposed isolationist foreign policy. Three months later the United States declared war on Spain and quickly defeated the antiquated Spanish fleet and army in engagements ranging from the Caribbean to the Philippines. Eight months after the war had begun, Spain's surrender left the United States in possession of a worldwide empire that spanned half the globe. Guam and Puerto Rico became (and still are) U.S. possessions, and the Philippines were granted independence after 15 years of guerrilla warfare against its U.S. liberators and existed 33 more years as a protectorate.

Cuba's resulting status was more complicated, and it draws an important parallel to understanding Panama's situation as it developed vis-à-vis the United States a decade later. After the Spanish-American War, Cuba was granted what political scientist Clifford Staten has called "conditional independence."[5] Though Cubans had been fighting for independence against Spain for decades, they were dismayed to find out that after Spain's defeat the United States would essentially replace it as a colonial power. In 1902, Cuba was given nominal independence, but that occasion was tempered by three important limitations on its sovereignty.

First, the previous year the United States had forced the Platt Amendment into the new Cuban constitution. This stipulated that the United States had the right to intervene militarily in Cuba if the island did not maintain "an adequate government," which meant any situation that ran counter to U.S. strategic interest. Second, 90 percent of the island's famed cigar industry and 60 percent of its all-important sugar industry was owned by American firms, which left the most powerful economic engines in Cuba in the hands of Americans. Lastly, the United States established the Guantánamo Bay naval base under a treaty that required that both sides had to agree in order to terminate the agreement. As we shall see, these types of arrangements were essentially the blueprints for the forthcoming arrangement with Panama.

The maintenance of such an array of territories forced policymakers in Washington to reconsider ways to solidify the U.S. newly won superpower status. Based on the dominant strategic theories of Alfred Thayer Mahan, a canal to join the two oceans emerged as an absolute necessity to maintain the war's gains. During the war, the battleship *Oregon*, stationed in the Puget Sound (Seattle) had received an urgent reinforcement call to the Caribbean to engage expected Spanish reinforcements. It completed a record-breaking, full-steam voyage, taking 60 days at 13 knots to round South America and reach Cuba. This incident solidified the need

for a canal more than any other single event, because now with possessions in both the Atlantic and Pacific, the two-ocean navy of the United
States had to be able to transfer forces quickly between the Atlantic and
Pacific Oceans. A canal was now seen as imperative to U.S. foreign policy,
and it was going to be constructed through a Central American country
one way or another.

NOTES

1. Hispanic surnames generally use the paternal and maternal last
names, in that order. But some Hispanics, like Balboa and Picasso, have
broken tradition and used only the maternal surname.

2. The term "Spanish America" specifically refers to the colonies settled
by Spain and therefore excludes Portuguese-settled Brazil, which did not
rebel against the motherland. After remaining a Portuguese colony until
1808, Brazil became a separate kingdom in 1815 under Portugal's King
Dom João, who had fled Napoléon's invasion, and afterwards was the
independent Brazilian Empire under João's son, Pedro, from 1833 to 1889.

3. Michael Conniff, *Panama and the United States: The Forced Alliance*
(Athens: University of Georgia Press, 1992), 23.

4. David McCullough, *The Path Between the Seas: The Creation of the Panama Canal, 1870–1914* (New York: Simon & Schuster, 1977), 148.

5. Clifford L. Staten, *The History of Cuba* (Westport, CT: Greenwood
Press, 2003), 40.

3

Completing the Canal to World War II

The completion of the Panama Canal was the capstone project that would define Panama from that point onward. It also signaled the beginning of an almost 100-year relationship between Panama and the United States that would run the gamut from intervention and repression to reconciliation and cooperation. The resulting relationship would deeply affect both countries' domestic politics. Though it is true that Panamanians had worked and struggled for independence from Colombia prior to the arrival of the United States, it is also true that Panama's birth as an independent nation was tainted by collusion, secret negotiations, and foreign actors. For the United States, the canal as seen as the next logical step in the U.S. expansion as a continental and commercial world power following the Spanish-American War of 1898. However, the construction of the canal would build more than just a waterway; it would eventually forge a nation.

ALMOST A CANAL

The bankruptcy of Lesseps's canal company seemingly removed the hope of a Panamanian canal for the near future, leaving the Colombian department of Panama with a useless 20-kilometer-long gouge in the earth. Panama's hopes lay in the French holders of the company's assets, who were desperately trying to find a buyer. But hopes for a Panamanian canal were doubly dashed by a bill considered in the U.S. Senate in 1900 that was to approve the construction of a U.S. canal in Nicaragua, ignoring the Clayton-Bulwer Treaty of 1850. A U.S. company, the Nicaraguan Canal Association, had already tried to begin a canal in 1889 but only finished a kilometer of the dig before going bankrupt. Nonetheless, a Nicaraguan canal now seemed to be closer to reality since Nicaragua was closer to the United States, and therefore the total transportation distance from coast to coast would be lessened. It also had the advantage of not possessing the financial and political "baggage" present in Panama.

The key figure who helped to change minds in the U.S. Senate was Frenchman Phillipe Bunau-Varilla, who had been Lesseps's chief engineer. Bunau-Varilla had invested much of his personal capital in a Panamanian canal and spent most of the 1890s trying to find investors to complete the canal. In 1899 he traveled to Washington to lobby politicians with favorable statistics and information on Panama and succeeded in convincing key senators to shelve the Nicaragua bill. He and a New York partner, William Nelson Cromwell, then convinced the French holding company to sell the Panama Canal's assets to the United States for $40 million, but not enough senators were swayed to have the measure passed. The U.S. Congress responded by passing the Spooner Act in June 1902, which authorized the amount to purchase French rights to canal and set the further condition that if the Colombian government failed to provide the land necessary for construction, then the United States would begin negotiations with Nicaragua. The bidding war between the two sites was fierce, and there were many in the U.S. Congress who were convinced that Nicaragua was the best option.

The turning point involved Nicaragua's active volcanoes near the proposed canal route. The Nicaraguan government had vehemently denied that there was active volcanism in the area. Just before a Senate vote that would decide the ultimate canal route, Bunau-Varilla played his trump card by sending senators recently issued Nicaraguan postage stamps showing Mount Monotombo, an active volcano situated near the proposed canal route, its fumaroles clearly belching black smoke. The Panama route won out over Nicaragua, and the bill authorized President Roosevelt to acquire the right of way and property of the old French company. The United States offered Colombia $10 million, plus $250,000 in annual payments. This offer was followed by a series of menacing telegraphs to the Colombian Congress that meant to intimate it into ratifying the agreement.

But the Colombians were not intimidated. The matter was hotly contested in the Colombian Congress and held up in debate for almost a year on the assumption that the United States could be persuaded to pay more. Seeing their opportunity fading, Panamanians began to float rumors of revolt against Bogotá if the treaty were not approved. The first organized meeting to consider independence from Colombia was held in July 1901. Many of the family names represented among the participants—Arango, Arias, Arosemena, and Boyd—were to become Panama's political as well as economic elite for the next 60 years. One member of this group, a physician from the bankrupt isthmian railroad, Manuel Amador, was selected to be the first president. He was sent to the United States to seek financial support and assurances from the U.S. government for Panamanian independence. But guarantees were not forthcoming from the new U.S. president, Theodore Roosevelt, who still sought to broker a deal with Colombia, even though he considered Colombians "contemptible little creatures" and berated them for blocking what he termed "a major highway of civilization." With typical disdainful bravado, Roosevelt is said to have quipped "we are dealing with a government of irresponsible bandits." He considered invading the isthmus to finish the canal, but thought it likely that there would soon be a revolution in Panama that would make intervention unnecessary.

Panamanians continued to chomp at the Colombian bit, and military rule by Colombia of the isthmus became the standard practice. Even the department's representatives in the Colombian government lived in Bogotá, not Panama, and all officials that governed Panama were likewise from Bogotá. Millions of pesos in taxes squeezed each year from the isthmus were in turn spent on supporting the Colombian soldiers who maintained order on the isthmus. In January 1895, Panama erupted in a rebellion that was suppressed by an overwhelming force of Colombian troops three months later. In 1898 the new Colombian president, Manuel Antonio Sanclemente, was elected with the opposition boycotting the vote. Sanclemente soon found his position tenuous, as he was unable to control his own party and hold the opposition in check.

The French Canal Company, whose 1878 concession would expire in 1904, offered Colombia $1 million for a renewal because it wanted to recoup part of its losses by selling off its right to the United States. Sanclemente's government was poised to accept, but the opposition and even the conservative Colombian Congress insisted on the French forfeiting their rights. As Sanclemente's administration rapidly lost prestige, Colombia's discontented opposition saw its opportunity, and a brutal civil war erupted. Called the Thousand Days' War, it was the most terrible and destructive that Colombia had ever experienced, and as usual, Panama was relegated to the periphery.

The tempest in Panama actually began brewing at the end of the civil war in 1902. Under the terms of the earlier agreement with Colombia, the United States had not only kept order on the isthmus but had provided the battleship on which the peace agreement was signed to end the civil war. By this time, as Panamanian historian Ricaurte Soler notes, Panamanians' national consciousness was fully developed, and Panama's elites were eager to finally make a clear break from Colombia.[1] With Colombia in disarray, Panamanians on the verge of revolt, and Roosevelt's administration eager for rights to finish the canal, a hurricane of opportunity was forming over the isthmus.

CREATING INDEPENDENCE AND A CANAL

Independence came to Panama in 1903, not with revolutionary glory but through deft diplomacy, tactics, and tricks. With so much financial interest at stake, Phillipe Bunau-Varilla had never let the idea of a Panamanian canal leave his thoughts. He met with Amador in New York in late 1902 while the future Panamanian president was seeking money for the coming revolution. Bunau-Varilla convincingly portrayed himself as a representative of the Roosevelt administration, though in fact he had no official recognition other than having met twice with the president to discuss the matter. In a masterful ploy, he promised Amador $100,000 and U.S. naval support for the rebellion if the new Republic of Panama would appoint him as its representative in Washington. Though the idea of a Frenchman being Panama's first foreign minister was distasteful, it was less so than the idea of another Panamanian revolt failing. Amador agreed, and the stage was set for revolution.

The United States had previously intervened in Panama on various occasions to uphold security in accordance with the 1846 treaty with Colombia. Panamanian secessionists had typically been viewed by Washington as a threat to American financial and strategic interests. Under the terms of the Hay-Pauncefote Treaty of 1901, Britain, diverted by its growing rivalry with Germany, gave the United States the latitude necessary to develop the canal. The U.S. Navy progressively became an arbiter between rival Colombian factions in the region, but still sought to maintain at least nominal Colombian sovereignty over the isthmus.

The U.S. Navy's arrival in 1903 instead ended up protecting Panamanians from Colombian reprisals. The *USS Nashville* arrived off Panama's coast on November 2, one day before the Colombian warship *Cartegena*, which carried 2,500 reinforcements. The *Nashville*, however, did not intervene against the Colombians, because its commander had not yet received orders countermanding the 1846 treaty. Those orders did arrive the next day, and a small contingent of U.S. Marines landed to secure the railroad depot in Colón, though they were outnumbered 10-to-1 by the Colombians. A U.S. railroad engineer cleverly convinced the Colombian commander to go alone to Panama City, promising that his troops would follow. After the Colombian commander's arrival in Panama City, the Panamanians, without the weaponry or the U.S. reinforcements necessary to defeat the Colombians militarily, resorted to bribing the Colombian commander and his troops, cleaning out all the banks in Panama to do so. To concretize the change, U.S. reinforcements finally arrived two days later on both coasts, and the Colombian troops were ignominiously ferried back to Colombia on a British mail steamer.

Only five shots were fired by the Colombians during the brief revolution, resulting in just one death, that of an elderly Chinese man.[2] Amid vociferous protests from Colombia that the United States had broken the 1846 treaty, the United States formally recognized the new country of Panama on November 13, justifying its actions under the provisions of the 1846 Bidlack-Mallarino treaty, which provided for the U.S. military to maintain transit open on the isthmus. For the rest of the year, Colombia rattled its saber and pleaded with European countries for assistance to retrieve Panama while the United States prepared for possible war. But by the beginning of the following year the whole affair was a fait accompli. Not until 1921 would Colombia be compensated by the United States with $21 million for the loss of Panama.

President Roosevelt's speedy recognition of the new Panamanian republic met with general approval within the United States, though it aroused some opposition among his political opponents who accused him of having schemed at the revolution for the purpose of obtaining the canal. But U.S. public opinion was on Roosevelt's side. Since the Spanish-American War, the need for a canal had become a strategic and commercial necessity. The building of the canal, the establishment of a Panamanian protectorate, and the tacit acquiescence of Europe to the action signaled the hegemony of the United States on a much greater scale than the previously unenforceable Monroe Doctrine had. Roosevelt later proclaimed that the arrogation of the isthmus was morally justified for the "sake of civilization."

The reception in Panama was more complicated. Panama's new elite was a hodgepodge that included Dr. Manuel Amador, José Agustín Arango, Ricardo Arias, Frederico Boyd, and Tomás Arias. For the next 60 years these men and their progeny would dominate Panamanian politics.

After a bit of wrangling and bravado, Bunau-Varilla received his diplomatic papers from the new Panamanian junta composed of Amador, Pablo Arosemena, and late-comer José Domingo de Obaldía, a Colombian official who had defected to the revolutionaries' cause. The junta instructed Bunau-Varilla that no agreement should be made with Washington that would compromise Panama's newly won freedom and that the junta must be consulted on any canal treaty.

Nonetheless, the Frenchman set out to fulfill his own agenda of getting a canal contract. Bunau-Varilla took up residence in New York's recherché Waldorf-Astoria and studied diplomatic law, wrote a Panamanian declaration of independence and a constitution, and even designed a flag for the incipient republic. Unbeknownst to the new Panamanian government, a few days later in Washington, D.C., Bunau-Varilla negotiated a new canal agreement with U.S. Secretary of State John Hay. Realizing the tremendous opportunity before him, Hay signed the treaty with little delay. The treaty was presented by Bunau-Varilla to Panama's new leaders, who were confronted with a difficult dilemma. The agreement essentially stripped the new government of much of its newly won sovereignty, but Panama's leaders understood the implicit but clear message that rejecting the treaty would mean a return to Colombia and a certain appointment in front of a firing squad for Panama's new leaders. Too late, Amador and Boyd were finally told that Bunau-Varilla had been overplaying his influence, but the bluff had run its course. On February 6, 1904, the Hay-Bunau-Varilla treaty was signed by Panama and went into force.

The United States acquired use of the Canal Zone across Panama for a one-time payment of $10 million and annual payments of $250,000. Even though early twentieth-century textbooks in the United States would claim otherwise, the United States never purchased the land outright and did not own the canal. On paper, the canal was still Panamanian but under U.S. control and management. In practice, however, the Canal Zone was treated by the United States as sovereign territory over which U.S. law and power were supreme. The treaty changed the extent of authority that the United States would exercise in the Canal Zone. Derived from the old Hay-Herrán treaty, it altered the arrangement so as to give the United States sovereignty "in perpetuity" instead of using the previous 99-year term limit. Within the Canal Zone, the United States would have the authority to act "as if it were sovereign" and was allowed to appropriate lands as necessary to bring the canal to completion. In a practical sense, the Panama Canal Zone had become an extension of U.S. territory and Panama City, though the capital of the country was under the eminent domain of the United States and thus subject to frequent U.S. intervention.

From the beginning, Panama's independence was nominal, because the newly established strip of U.S.-controlled territory surrounding the Canal Zone divided the country in half. Similar to the Platt Amendment imposed on Cuba three years before, the Hay-Bunau-Varilla treaty's ambiguous language gave the United States broad latitude to intervene in Panamanian domestic affairs. The United States promised to guarantee Panama's independence, but Article 7 of the treaty pronounced that "the same right and authority are granted to the United States for the maintenance of public order." A second addition, Article 136, was so inflammatory that it almost caused a popular uprising. It stipulated that the United States could intervene militarily in Panama if the United States thought it necessary to maintain order. This arrangement meant that Panama's sovereign was severely restricted and set up a system where two governments operated within the country: one for Panama and one for the Canal Zone. Panama's new Liberal party opposed the stipulation, but the Conservatives supported it.

With its most valuable potential revenue-maker out of its hands, Panama became to a great degree economically dependent on the United States. Until 1936, when the Canal treaty was first revised, the isthmus existed in a legal-political limbo as a protectorate of the United States.

In three important ways, the United States began to exercise hegemony over the isthmus. First, a dual-tier payroll system was implemented. During the building of the Panama Canal, Americans were paid in gold coin with copious fringe benefits, while some 45,000 laborers—mostly Panamanian and West Indian with a large minority of Southern Europeans—were paid in less-valuable silver coin with no benefits. This practice continued until the late 1940s when the payroll switched to paper currency and the Americans simply earned more while Panamanians earned less.

Second, the growing influence of the U.S. on Panamanian life was manifested by the imposition of Jim Crow laws in the Canal Zone and, in general, a paternalistic disdain for Panamanians. Many of the canal supervisors were Southerners only one generation removed from the U.S. Civil War who had brought with them the typical racist attitudes of the time. Also similar to the U.S. South at the time, the Canal Zone saw the emergence of separate public facilities, Panamanians working in the Canal Zone saw "whites only" signs begin to appear in every facet of public life, from restrooms to water fountains. Even the Panama's presidency was not immune to U.S. racism. In 1910, Vice President Carlos Mendoza, a mulatto, was expected to win the upcoming election. The U.S. Chief of Mission in Panama, Richard Marsh, threatened military action if Mendoza were elected. Mendoza quietly withdrew from the race. In their own country, Panamanians were treated as second-class citizens.

Lastly, with the Monetary Convention of 1904, the U.S. dollar was made legal tender in Panama—a practice that continues to this day. By accepting this arrangement, the Panamanian government's hands were tied, since it could not make any monetary policy on its own. The end result of these changes was the "Panama Canal Zone," a 16-by-80-kilometer-wide area in which U.S. culture and law were paramount. In the "Zone," as it came to be known, American food, music, housing, and entertainment—even bowling alleys—were omnipresent and stood in stark contrast to the Panamanian culture outside the Zone. "Zonians," as the U.S. residents were known, lived in a quasi-utopian paradise. Practically everything was subsidized by the U.S. government, crime was low, and for multiple generations many Americans would spend a good part of their lives "in the Zone" living as if they were back in the States.

However, the close proximity and the omnipresent influence of U.S. mass consumerism would forever alter economic attitudes among Panamanians. For example, unlike their Central American neighbors, Panamanians quickly developed high-consumption preferences that a lesser-developed state like Panama could not sustain on its own, thus reinforcing the country's dependence on the United States.

In sum, the treaty gave the United States hegemony in Panama, and Panama's government had no choice but to accept the situation. The treaty was part of a larger U.S. policy direction called the Roosevelt Corollary in which Panama was an integral component. Based on the Monroe Doctrine, the United States began to exercise "international police power" in the Western Hemisphere in the early twentieth century and additionally sought to "civilize" Latin American nations by stationing U.S. troops to "make them fulfill their obligation" and "elect good men." Roosevelt himself best explained the supplement when he said, in reference to U.S. intervention in Latin America, "We would interfere with them only in the last resort, and then only if it became evident that their inability or unwillingness to do justice at home and abroad had violated the rights of the United States and invited foreign aggression to the detriment of the entire body of American nations." The moral mission also had a broader geopolitical goal: to prevent the Kaiser's Germany from establishing a foothold in the Caribbean Basin, particularly in Panama.

Simultaneously, a new political nation as well as a new waterway was created in Panama. In January 1904, representatives from all over Panama drew up a democratic constitution modeled largely on the U.S. Constitution. As previously agreed, Amador was elected by Panama's new assembly as the nation's first president, and two political parties emerged to contend for the upcoming election in 1904. Amador's Conservative

Party was principally the political vehicle of Panama's small but influential white minority elite. Opposing them was the Liberal Party, which primarily represented the country's majority mestizos and mulattos. However, Panama's politicians had no experience in the art of compromise necessary for successful democracy, and very soon a coup plot was being hatched by the Liberals.

To head off any instability that might disrupt the construction of the canal, the Canal Zone's U.S. governor, George W. David, demanded that Panama's small military force disband and that all Panamanian munitions be put under U.S. supervision. In its place and to counter further coup-making, the United States assumed responsibility for training the Panamanian police force, giving it a U.S. superintendent. While offensive to ordinary Panamanians' national pride, U.S. control over the means of force did resolve a central political difficulty that confronted Panama's small oligarchy. Since Panama's economy depended more on trade than agriculture, the mostly urban and mercantile oligarchy held little real political control over its own, largely rural, population. Therefore, the elites' intimate relationship with the United States allowed them to exercise control beyond what should have been the case.

Given the U.S. determination that nothing impede the canal's construction, the elites quickly learned that the United States could be counted on to put down dissent. But in the end, the United States was doubly beneficial to Panama's oligarchy. It provided internal stability and security but, simultaneously, the overwhelming U.S. presence fostered resentment, which the elite used to create the nationalism that would politically and economically unite the country.

JOINING THE TWO SEAS

To facilitate construction, the United States built what amounted to a city along the canal's route. Offices, construction shacks, hospitals, and housing quarters arose along with a government structure that included police and fire departments, courts, customs houses, and a post office. Initially allocating $40 million to the project, Roosevelt assigned direction of construction to the U.S. Army Corps of Engineers, with Col. George Washington Goethals as director of the newly established Panama Canal Commission.

Roosevelt's orders to Goethals were simple: "Make the dirt fly." Preparations began in May 1904, though actual construction would not begin for another three years. Whereas de Lesseps had planned a sea-level canal, the United States opted for series of locks to surmount the problem posed by Panama's mountains, and the key component was the Culebra Cut (later renamed Gaillard Cut), which connected Lake Gatún with the Atlantic-side locks. Though only 14 kilometers long, this segment of the canal took six years and 6,000 workers to get through, with the shortest mountain in the country, which stood 150 meters tall, blocking the path. Over 9 million kilos of dynamite were used to remove 96 million cubic meters of mountain. To fill the canal, the Chagres River was dammed to create Lake Gatún, making it during the early twentieth century the world's largest artificial lake. American engineers used more than 23 million kilos of TNT to finish the canal and employed over one thousand steam shovels and hundreds of thousands of pick-axes along the route.

Like their French counterparts, U.S. builders were confronted with the looming specter of disease as well as the mammoth engineering challenges. A 1905 *Harper's Magazine* cartoon shows Teddy Roosevelt and Uncle Sam viewing a skull-shaped mountain of yellow fever, calling it "the first mountain to be removed" before canal construction could proceed. However, in the intervening years between the French and U.S. efforts, medical science had progressed greatly. The French had believed that yellow fever was caused by poisonous gases from wetlands and was passed from person to person through sewage, filth, and decaying animal carcasses. Though several scientific papers in the mid-1800s had refuted this assumption, the first conclusive evidence that mosquitoes were the disease's carriers was provided in 1881 by a Cuban doctor, Carlos Juan Finley. This proved to be significant, because it was common practice, dating from the French effort, to put hospital bed legs in pans of water to prevent ants from climbing onto malaria patients. These open water sources were, of course, the perfect breeding ground for mosquitoes.

Nonetheless, Finley's work was ignored by U.S. officials until a U.S. army doctor, William Crawford Gorgas, tested Finley's proposals in Cuba following the Spanish-American War of 1898. Following Finley's recommendations, malaria was reduced by over 80 percent in Havana. Because of his success in Cuba, Gorgas was transferred to Panama, where he immediately implemented an expanded version of Finley's program that included the drainage of all standing water, including wells, and replaced the obsolete water system with aqueducts. Additionally, every house and store in Panama City was fumigated, the streets were paved, mosquito netting was erected over windows and doors, and 250,000 liters of oil per month were spread onto areas of standing water. By the end of 1905, malaria had been eradicated in Panama City and in the canal work zone. But in its place, pneumonia became the main killer, primarily due to the constantly wet working conditions typical of the tropics. Over the course of the construction the Panama Canal Commission listed 4,513 deaths due to disease, but like the French experience, many workers undoubtedly died outside the purview of official record keepers, so the real total was probably much higher.

The other area in which the America effort mirrored the French was in the chronic labor shortage. According to Panamanian historian Alfredo Castillero Calvo, workers came from 97 different countries. By 1912, there were over 45,000 workers, including 30,000 Caribbean blacks (mostly Jamaicans), 2,000 Italians, and 1,100 Greeks. Panama had become a "new Babel."[3] There were more foreign workers in the canal work zone than Panamanians in Panama City and Colón combined, and among them Caribbean blacks, in particular, found life especially difficult.

The blacks were discriminated against on two fronts. Bigoted Americans, including Goethals himself, held nothing but contempt for the Caribbean blacks. The Panama Canal Commission typically recorded official remarks that classified blacks as unqualified for higher salaries, and based on the assumption of racial differentiation, blacks were frequently used to test new chemical agents, such as DDT. Panamanians, on the other hand, resented the blacks' superior numbers, which had caused housing prices to soar. Caribbean blacks were also seen as "invaders," since they were largely Protestants and English speakers. Clashes between blacks and Panamanians were frequent, as were occasional murders. By the end of construction, due to worker turnover, more than 250,000 men had labored to build the canal.

In late 1913, President Woodrow Wilson pressed a button in Washington that signaled the opening of the gates holding back the Chagres River. Lake Gatún filled, and the Panama Canal became a reality. In August 1914 the first ship to use the canal was the concrete ship *Cristóbal*, but the first official, publicized crossing was made by the ship *Ancon*. All told, the final cost to the United States to build the canal was $367 million ($6.5 billion in 2003 dollars), and more than 183 million cubic meters of earth had been moved. But, since the canal was completed just prior to the outbreak of World War I, traffic was unexpectedly low for the canal's first four years of operation. However, the war's end meant a four-fold increase in traffic. In the canal's first year of operation, 4.5 million metric tons of cargo crossed the isthmus. This amount would increase exponentially to 152 million metric tons a year by the end of the twentieth century.

BUILDING A NATION

Panama's leaders expected to be treated as the government representatives of a sovereign nation, but the unequal relationship caused them disappointment from the outset. From the beginning, Panama's political system was molded by the United States to promote the Conservative government, which had allied itself with U.S. interests. Any political challenge to the Conservatives was met by U.S. military force. Within one year of independence, Panama's young military, under the command of a former Colombian officer, Esteban Huertas, threatened a takeover in October 1904 in reaction to proposed reductions in military expenditures. But a cable sent by Panamanian president Amador to U.S. president Roosevelt brought a quick end to the crisis with the landing of U.S. Marines. The Conservatives became quite good at playing on U.S. fears of instability to their own benefit.

Only four years later, during Panama's second national election in 1908, the Conservatives disseminated propaganda of uprisings to rouse the United States into sending troops into the country to supervise the elections. In 1913, in an effort to prevent the Panamanian police from helping the Liberals, the United States demanded that the Panamanian police relinquish their high-power rifles, leaving Panama's domestic security to men who had only pistols. Despite strong opposition to the growing U.S. civilian and military presence, the Conservatives quietly acquiesced to the steady buildup of a permanent U.S. military presence within the Canal Zone. The United States began to use its Panama bases as the launching point for military interventions in other countries, particularly Nicaragua. Also noteworthy is the fact that the Canal Zone became at this time one of the U.S. military's primary storage facilities and testing grounds for conventional ordinance as well as chemical weapons. The Río Hato Air Force Base in southern Panama was converted into a test site for human experimentation. The Canal Zone itself would remain a repository for chemical weapons until the end of the 1980s. In particular, one island off Panama's coast, San José Island, was left so littered with mustard gas containers that it is still known as a chemical weapons wasteland.[4]

By the end of World War I, there were 14 U.S. bases in the Zone containing 7,400 U.S. soldiers. From this central position, and at the request of subsequent Conservative governments, U.S. troops entered Panama City and other parts of the country to quell riots as well as Liberals' protests. In 1925, striking workers complaining about increased rents were met by 600 U.S. soldiers' bayonets, killing many Panamanians. While effective in maintaining Conservatives' control, continued dependence on the United States stripped the oligarchy of any political legitimacy.

Panama's financial independence was also short lived. Since Panama had no established banks, after 1914 the American financial institutions National Bank and Chase National established offices in Panama City. Soon they had compelled Panama's young government to give them financial oversight of major economic sectors such as the railroad and some agricultural production zones. The onset in 1929 of the Great Depression further intensified Panama's dependence on the United States. The revenue generated from trade with the 40,000 Americans living in the Canal Zone at times represented 90 percent of all Panamanian exports, which amounted to one-third of Panama's gross national product.

Continued intervention and interference in Panama by the United States as well as the steady growth of popular opposition to the original terms of the treaty finally brought minor concessions from Washington. The treaty's original language obliged Panama to consider itself at war whenever the United States was, and allowed the U.S. military to conduct maneuvers outside the Canal Zone during peacetime. In 1927 the Panamanian assembly rose up in protest, vociferously denying that the United States had such rights to infringe on Panama's sovereignty. Panama even appealed to the League of Nations, but was ignored. The United States finally announced a policy change in 1928 when President Herbert Hoover declared in his "Good Neighbor Policy" that the United States would no longer intervene in Latin America.

Perhaps to test, if not take advantage of, the new policy, in 1931 a secretive, nationalist civilian group called Acción Comunal (Communal Action), with support from the National Police, forced President Florencio Harmodio Arosemena to resign. Led by the populist Arnulfo Arias, the group reflected broad-based discontent among Panama's professionals—engineers, lawyers, bureaucrats, and other professionals—whose jobs were being taken by Americans in canal-related administration. Publicly, the United States did not openly condemn the action since the Hoover administration's approach was to distance itself from the "gunboat diplomacy" of Teddy Roosevelt and Woodrow Wilson. But the coup's success was ultimately guaranteed with a promise by Arias to Washington that U.S. interests would not be threatened.

Arnulfo's older brother, Harmodio, was installed as acting president, marking the first time a mestizo had broken the rotating cycle of white elites who had held the presidency since independence. A graduate of the London School of Economics, Harmodio had gained fame in Panama from a book he authored that assailed the intent and practice of the Monroe Doctrine. He was openly elected as president the following year, and his administration was characterized by public works projects targeted at the middle and lower classes, including the founding of the University of Panama and poverty relief programs in the outlying countryside as well as the unification of nationalist forces in Panama against the overwhelming U.S. presence. The following decade was one of reactionary nationalist rule that appealed to the middle class and undermined the power of the elite. But the United States did not interfere, since Harmodio was deemed "responsible" by Washington.

The actions of this so-called "Generation of '31" demonstrated that, without the support of the United States, the oligarchy could not maintain control of the country through open elections. Of great help to increasing Panama's autonomy steadily throughout the 1930s was Franklin D. Roosevelt's "Good Neighbor Policy." A continuation of the early Hoover administration's non-intervention policy, it emphasized political friendship along with economic leverage. The last important factor to Panama's greater autonomy was the well-founded U.S. fears of growing German and Japanese trade in Panama as well as agents seeking inroads in the isthmus.

The interwar years were characterized by an economic downturn and political upheaval. In 1934, the U.S. dollar was devalued by 40 percent, which reduced the annual $250,000 canal payment to Panama by an equal proportion. To protest the loss of income, the Panamanian government began refusing the payment. Finally, amid the fear of growing Axis infiltration in the isthmus, Panama was able to leverage itself for certain concessions, including the end of U.S. supervision of its National Police. For the first time, a Panamanian, José Antonio Remón, became the head of the police. Remón was chosen since he was the only Panamanian with professional military training, having graduated from the Mexican Military Academy.

From 1934 to 1937, Panama passed various tariff laws meant to provide some protection for domestic industrial production. However, Panamanian merchants' dependence on sales to the Canal Zone attenuated the call for a more independent trade policy. In the end, Panama's efforts to develop an independent industrial base after the Great Depression were only minimally successful, making it easily the most externally dependent country in Latin America.

The capstone to Panama's demands was the Hull-Alfaro Treaty of 1936, which ended Panama's status as a protectorate of the United States. Though some in the U.S. Congress and the U.S. War Department protested, complained, and delayed votes, the treaty was finally signed in 1939 on the eve of World War II. The United States renounced the right to seize Panamanian land without consent, and the U.S. right to intervention was abrogated. In addition, the annual payment to Panama was increased to $430,000, though as Walter LaFeber notes, the increase was deceptively little since the dollar's previous devaluation meant an actual increase of only $7,500.[5]

The new treaty also stipulated that the future security of the canal was to be a joint endeavor, though the U.S. military still retained the ability to conduct maneuvers outside the Canal Zone. Lastly, the United States promised to create a more equitable pay scale. Though temporarily satisfying to Panamanians' sense of national pride, the treaty ultimately did not address what Panamanians sought most—direct ownership over the canal itself. This crusade would occupy the Panamanian public consciousness for the next 61 years.

THE RISE AND FALL OF ARNULFO ARIAS

Arnulfo Arias, now head of the right-wing National Revolutionary Party, was elected president in 1938. A Harvard-educated physician, Arias was supported by a new coalition of middle-class and some upper-class Panamanians and was elected by an unprecedented majority. After a visit to Nazi Germany in 1937, Arias had emerged as an ardent nationalist. His political acumen rested in his deep understanding of Panamanians' frustration with the U.S. occupation. Arias's rallying cry became *panameñismo*, which roughly meant "Panama for Panamanians" and implied a desire to expel all non-Panamanians from the country.

However, in addition to the carrot of nationalism that he offered to the public, Arias also wielded an equally effective stick. To tighten his grip on power, he utilized authoritarian measures such as jailing dissidents, subverting newspapers, and disenfranchising Panama's non-Spanish-speaking population, particularly the English-speaking Jamaican population. In 1941, Arias pushed a new constitution through the largely subservient National Assembly in which the president's term was to be extended and created the National Secret Police, which was chartered to be independent of the National Police. The additional insult to the National Police was the appointment of a Guatemalan army officer as Panama's inspector general, which created an irreparable schism between Arias and the National Police.

While his heavy-handed methods certainly created animosity, Arias's message did strike a chord among middle-class Panamanians, a group that benefited from the U.S. presence but nonetheless felt restricted. Nationalism and radical reform in social areas had become central themes for most of Panama's population. However, in the end it was Arias's expression of admiration and even allegiance with the Nazis that finally brought the United States back to intervention, though indirectly. Arias had rebuffed U.S. requests to renew the 999-year leases on military bases and had refused to arm Panamanian-registered ships during the war, which Arias claimed violated their neutrality. This disturbed U.S. policymakers, who were already apprehensive about his public pro-Nazi sentiments and viewed him as a possible threat to the canal's security.

While Arias was secretly in Cuba visiting his mistress in October 1941, Rogelio Fábrega, the National Police's second-in-command, reported the president's absence, and orders were made for the arrests of Arias's supporters. The Panamanian Supreme Court declared the presidency vacant, therefore justifying Arias's replacement. The National Police carried out the coup against Arias and was tacitly supported by the United States as well as Arias's own brother, Harmodio. Ricardo Adolfo de la Guardia was installed as a caretaker president, and Arias went into exile in Argentina.

Supported by the oligarchy, the military, and opponents of Arias's neofascism, de la Guardia's government sided with the United States once war arrived in December 1941. The United States was given 134 sites throughout the country to use as military bases. In the eight years following Arias's ouster (1941–1949), six presidents held office, one for less than day, which showcases the turbulent state of the country's politics and the insecurity of the armed forces with civilian leadership. But, more ominously, the coup marked the beginning of a tumultuous chapter in Panama's history, signaling the escalation of the direct involvement the country's armed forces and its emersion as the ultimate arbiter in isthmian society.

Political turbulence aside, the war ended up being a prosperous time for Panama, even though the conflict greatly reduced commercial traffic, the buildup of U.S. forces, the passage of convoys, and defense-related construction sustained the economy. In the interest of defense, roads were improved between Panama City and Colón, the canal's third locks were finished, and the resultant U.S. spending produced as much revenue as the original canal construction project. Also, from 1939 to 1941 the Neutrality Act provided a great incentive for U.S. shipping and oil companies to register their ships in Panama to take advantage of continued business with Britain. The first to do so was Standard Oil Company, but after the war ended, the laxity of Panamanian law regarding taxes, labor, and safety regulations meant that the country would become the single largest titular home of the world's ocean-going fleets (by 1995, 13,717 ships were so registered).

NOTES

1. Ricaurte Soler, *Formas Ideológicas de la Nación Panameña* (San José, Costa Rica: EDUCA, 1972), 125.

2. Lester D. Langley, *The United States and the Caribbean in the Twentieth Century* (Athens: University of Georgia Press, 1989), 37.

3. Alfredo Castillero Calvo, *La ruta interoceánica y el canal de Panamá* (Panama City: Colegio Panameño de Historiadores e Instituto del Canal de Panamá y Estudios Internacionales, Universidad de Panamá, 1999), 118.

4. John Lindsay-Poland, *Emperors in the Jungle: The Secret History of the U.S. in Panama* (Durham, NC: Duke University Press, 2003), 64.

5. Walter LaFeber, *The Panama Canal: The Crisis in Historical Perspective,* updated ed. (New York: Oxford University Press, 1989), 69.

4

Panama during the Cold War

The end of World War II brought a number of important political and social changes to Panama. Wartime investment of $154 million created an economic boon, which then turned bust as U.S. postwar-related investment decreased. The country rapidly urbanized, as Panamanians migrated in droves to Panama City and Colón, creating housing and job shortages. By the end of the 1940s, about 40 percent of Panamanians lived in these two canal cities. Squalor, overcrowding, and unemployment were aggravated by a 2 percent downturn in per capita income.

But the greatest potential source of income, the canal, was still not lucrative for two reasons. First, Panama's portion of revenue from canal operations had not risen significantly since the canal's opening 31 years earlier. Second, Panamanian canal employees encountered a glass ceiling. Though Panamanians' educational level had risen substantially since independence, and a growing percentage of Panamanians were professionals in the service sector, the grapes of further prosperity hung tantalizingly out of reach, since the skilled, better-paying canal positions that Panamanians were now qualified to take were still not available to them.

The 1936 Hull-Alfaro treaty that had promised equal employment opportunity had gone unimplemented. Complaints to Washington during the war by Panama's government regarding continued racial discrimination in canal employment had made an impression on President Roosevelt, but it was not until the Panamanian government made citizens of the previously undesired West Indian blacks that Washington finally took notice. Giving the West Indians Panamanian citizenship effectively raised the volume of labor's voice in Panama to an unbearable level, much too high for Washington to ignore during wartime. The U.S. presence in the Zone continued to be a thorn in the side of most Panamanians, though since the canal's opening Panamanian merchants had profited through sales to U.S. forces. However, after the war these very same merchants now viewed the Canal Zone as unfair competition, since those Panamanians who did work in the Zone were able to buy many consumer goods cheaper at U.S. Canal Zone commissaries and outlets.

Symbolically, political change in postwar Panama came about in October 1945 when Arnulfo Arias, who had been in exile in Argentina, returned to a triumphant reception. Leaflets proclaiming *"¡Ya viene el hombre!"* (The man is coming soon!) covered Panama City, and Arias immediately began to rally support among the country's disgruntled small merchants, urban workers, and rural landholders for his bid in the 1948 presidential elections. At the same time, the National Police and the government prepared to ensure his defeat.

GROWING NATIONALISM

The rising level of discontent in Panama was amplified by geopolitical events elsewhere. In the post-World War II period, former European colonies in Africa and Asia began to achieve their independence. These new states' independence became an uncomfortable reminder to Panamanians of their quasi-colonial protectorate status under the United States. Both labor and the intelligentsia in Panama became more determined to challenge the U.S. dominance of the country.

This mounting rejection of the United States was further fueled by the *hispanidad* movement sweeping Latin America. Initially promoted as a neo-fascist ideology by Spain's dictator, Francisco Franco, *la hispanidad* envisaged a community of Hispanic nations with Spain as the model. However, the ideology largely found root in Latin America in a more innocuous form—the promotion and adoration for all things Hispanic and the implicit rejection of all that was not. With this added pride as the backdrop, the dominance of the United States within Panama stood in sharp relief.

This resurgent Panamanian nationalism contrasted greatly with the Panamanian government's official stance, which tended toward accommodation. During the last years of the war, President Ricardo Aldolfo de la Guardia's government had ruled by fiat, and his administration's intimate ties with Washington were perceived by many Panamanians as a sellout of Panama's sovereignty. He was forced out in 1945, and the National Assembly named Enrique Jiménez his successor.

With the war over, the U.S. military proposed keeping the over-100 military bases acquired in the 1942 agreement, which contained a clause for postwar renegotiation of the bases. But, under mounting domestic pressure, Panama's government demanded the land back. U.S. ambassador Frank T. Hines agreed to return more than 100 sites but counter offered with 20-year extensions on the Río Hato airbase and a dozen other sites. Over the objections of his foreign minister, President Jiménez authorized the measure and sent it to the National Assembly.

The news struck a particularly sensitive nerve among university students, communists, socialists, and, especially, the Arnulfistas (followers of Arias), all of whom expressed vociferous opposition to the U.S. presence. When the Assembly met in early December 1947 to consider the treaty renegotiation, its deliberations were interrupted by a riot. Led by a politically active university student group, the Frente Patriótico de la Juventud (Youth Patriotic Front), over 10,000 angry and armed Panamanians stormed the Assembly. Confronted by the National Police, a bloody melee ensued in which one student was killed and dozens were injured.

Amid such public ill-will, the Assembly voted unanimously to reject the U.S. offer. The United States abandoned the bases the following year, and also turned over control of Panama City's water and sewer systems, which had been under U.S. supervision since the canal's construction. The following year all civilian air traffic from Albrook Field in the Canal Zone was transferred to Panama's new international airport at Tocumen. This shockingly violent incident marked the first time a popular movement had foiled U.S. intentions in Panama and signaled an important turning point for domestic political relations.

The average Panamanian's dissatisfaction with the status quo had reached its limit, and the upsurge in demonstrations was the beginning of a long period of intense common hatred between demonstrators—particularly students—and the police, which mirrored a general shift in Panamanian society in the late 1940s. The street violence bred antagonism between the National Police and students, a tension that was to shade domestic Panamanian politics for the coming decades. The university students had become Panama's newest and loudest political actor, taking political deliberation out of the National Assembly and thrusting it into the streets through boisterous and, occasionally, violent protests.

In part, the mutual hatred was spawned by a social rift that had developed in Panamanian society. Under recruitment programs sponsored by the National Police, poorer blacks and mestizos from rural areas were finding avenues for social advancement in the police's ranks. By the 1940s, the police force was more representative of the lower classes while university students were increasingly middle class but less racially diverse. While not as overtly nationalistic as wealthier university students, who typically studied overseas, the middle class students found U.S. ownership of the Panama Canal a bitter pill to swallow. Many supported its outright nationalization by the Panamanian government.

THE RISE OF THE NATIONAL GUARD

The presidential elections in 1948 were the beginning of a confusing but important period of transition that was the beginning of a shift in political power toward the military and away from the weakened oligarchy, a change that would dominate Panama for the next 41 years. The elections pitted former president Arnulfo Arias against the Liberal, Domingo Díaz Arosemena, in an extremely close contest. The National Police were deployed, reputedly to monitor the elections, but their presence was really a calculated maneuver to influence the election's outcome against Arias. Though Arias received a slim winning margin of 1,500 votes, he was not allowed to take office. Driven by street rioting and an intense personal hatred of Arias, the head of the National Police, José Remón, made enough votes disappear to allow Díaz to edge out a win. Arias fled for Costa Rica, from where he tried, unsuccessfully, to mount an invasion of Panama.

Díaz Arosemena died in office the following year, and for the next three years, the National Police managed power, creating several short-term presidencies, which included three different presidents during November of 1949. The last of these presidents, Daniel Chanis, tried to break up Remón's lucrative cattle-slaughtering monopoly, which resulted in the president's resignation being obtained at the point of National Police rifles. The successor was Remón's cousin, Second Vice President Roberto Chiari. However, Chiari's bloodline was not sufficient to protect him. He sat as president for only one week before also being forced out by the police.

To everyone's astonishment, Remón then reinstalled Arnulfo Arias. Always a political chameleon and now on his best behavior, Arias was able to lull both Remón and the U.S. State Department into a false sense of security for a short time. But eventually Arias's autocratic tendencies overtook his self-discipline. In 1951, he jailed six former presidents, closed a newspaper, suspended the constitution and tried to dissolve the National Assembly. In addition, Arias and his family forced the owners of the best coffee plantations to sell out to him and developed an extensive narcotics-smuggling operation, led by the president's nephew, Antonio Arias, who become known among Panamanian pundits as "the druggist." Following a brief firefight with Arias supporters in which 16 people died, the National Police again deposed Arias. Though First Vice President Alcibíades Arosemena was installed as the new president, it was now Remón who made key policy decisions, which were implemented through the office of the president.

This second toppling of Arias marked the beginning of the Panamanian military's more direct intervention in domestic politics and a reduction in power of the oligarchy, which increasingly was seen as a helpless force between the vociferous university students and the brutal National Guard. Between 1948 and 1952 multiple presidents came and went with exceeding brevity of tenure, all installed by the National Guard's commander, José Antonio Remón.

THE FIRST BREAK WITH THE PAST

Raised in poverty, Remón had joined the police and risen through the ranks, eventually becoming the first Panamanian to receive formal professional training, at a military academy in Mexico. After becoming head of the National Police in 1947, he assumed two missions: to transform the police into a professional military force and to accumulate political power for himself.

In the first task, he changed the name of the National Police to the National Guard in 1953 and, assisted by U.S. military aid, armed the Guard with modern weaponry. Remón established the foundation for professional growth, exposing more than 600 soldiers and officers to formal military training. One officer of special note among this first generation of professionally trained officers was a medical school dropout named Manuel Antonio Noriega.

Remón also raised officers' salaries and engendered a true espirit d'corps by easing race relations among the enlisted mestizos and blacks. This anti-discrimination policy was significant since the National Guard became the only national institution that offered non-white young men an opportunity for social mobility in a country still dominated by a white oligarchy. Remón also encouraged other aspiring military men to follow his example and attend foreign military schools, since Panama had none. This professionalization increased the military's legitimacy to the populace while, at the same time, the civilian governments sharpened their own illegitimacy in the eyes of the public. With a more professional force at his disposal, Remón then utilized the more unified and powerful National Guard in his quest for political power.

Remón's importance as a central actor in Panamanian politics grew along with the fusion of *personalismo* (personalism) in the police force. A Hispanic political phenomenon, *personalismo* emphasized the charisma of the leader over the merits and quality of his leadership. In Panama, this approach previously had been relegated to civilian politics, since the top positions in the National Police had been awarded to loyal presidential supporters. Panamanian presidents' command over the National Police in the late 1930s and 1940s had made it an increasingly powerful political weapon against opponents and dissenters. As a result, this had altered the functioning of government in Panama City by decreasing the avenues of opposition versus "increasing well-entrenched executives." This forced the opposition into open conflict with the forces of government, frequently in the streets of Panama City.

The power of the National Guard was bolstered by U.S. fears of communist intrusion into Latin America. Panama's small but vocal Communist party, the Partido del Pueblo (People's Party), was kept muzzled by the Panamanian government's criminalization of its activities. The U.S. Military Defense Assistance Act of 1951 provided financial and training assistance to Latin American militaries for internal security, which supported the U.S. State Department's assessment that Latin America's food and raw materials were vital to the defense of the West. In the case of Panama, however, its importance was its strategic location and the canal.

The early 1950s were a time of significant economic change for the isthmus. Since its opening, the Canal Zone had existed as quasi-socialist entity—almost everything was subsidized for U.S. citizens in the Zone (called "Zonians") by the U.S. government, including housing, meals, and even vacations. But less than a half-century after its completion, the Panama Canal had begun to lose a portion of its usefulness. The French and American builders of the canal never could have envisioned the mammoth aircraft carriers and oil supertankers that would later ply the seas. These vessels were too large to pass through canal. Also, in the midst of a potential U.S.-Soviet conflict, the canal was highly vulnerable to modern weapons such as sub-launched missiles. These flaws degraded the canal's true operational value, thus removing some of the justification for maintaining such extravagant support for the Zone.

Calls for a more effective budget and more efficiency were met with great resistance by the Canal Zone's governor, Francis Newcomer, who ruled the Zone with an iron hand and consistently rejected all efforts to democratize and desegregate the canal. At one point, he was described as a person who "lacked human sympathy and justice."[1] But in 1951 the U.S. Congress passed a bill that reorganized the canal so that it would produce revenue for the U.S. government instead of vice versa. Two new agencies were created: the Panama Canal Company, which managed the canal's commercial operations and the Panama Railroad; and the Canal Zone government, which administered police, courts, and other nonmilitary areas. From this point on, all civilian canal operations were to be self-financed by tolls and other canal-related revenue sources. Though Zonians were negatively affected by the reorganization's austerity measures, Panamanians were doubly so, worsening the postwar recession because of the elimination of low-cost housing and social services for non-U.S. citizens.[2]

The austerity measures imposed on the Canal Zone meant a reciprocal downturn for Panama's economy, since the reduction of U.S. dollars in circulation meant fewer Panamanian balboas, which were really the same currency. The monetary contraction hit the 10,000 Panamanians employed in the Canal Zone especially hard. Equally distressful was the growing poor distribution of land in the isthmus. Though successive Panamanian administrations would claim to address the situation, the reality was that for the coming quarter-century, small land holders would be increasingly cut out of agricultural aid programs that tended to favor large estates oriented toward the export of bananas, sugar, coffee, and cattle.

Given the growing financial and security concerns surrounding the canal's future usefulness, a number of alternatives were explored by the United States, including the construction of a new canal either elsewhere in Panama or along previously explored routes in Nicaragua or in Mexico. The most ambitious, controversial, and, in hindsight, misguided proposal was to use nuclear explosives to excavate a new canal. Called Project Plowshare, the plan intended to use up to 300 nuclear charges to blast a canal out of the Darién jungle, which would have meant displacing upwards of 40,000 Kuna Indians from their lands. The idea was finally shelved when the group studying the project, the Interoceanic Canal Study Commission, determined that such means were not viable because radioactive fallout would contaminate Panama and perhaps even Colombia. Instead, the canal's Gaillard Cut was widened from 100 to 167 meters, the channel deepened, its curvy transit points straightened, and modern lighting added to allow 24-hour operation.

STEPS TOWARD SOVEREIGNTY

In 1952, Colonel Remón shed his uniform for the elections, becoming presidential candidate Remón. His subsequent victory was made possible through a deal with five parties to form one umbrella organization, the National Patriotic Coalition (CPN), and a good deal of vote manipulation via National Police pressure. The dubious nature of the victory was expressed by the opposition candidate, Roberto Chiari, who called Remón's election a "dangerous burlesque of democratic principles." Nonetheless, Remón's presidency was warmly greeted by the U.S. State Department, who viewed him as a reliable anti-communist.

On the other hand, Remón was no sycophant of the United States. A complicated figure, he was a committed nationalist and progressive but was also highly corrupt, using his office for personal gain. Remón portrayed himself as a reformer, touting a slogan of "peace, work, and bread." His administration increased both domestic social spending and economic development assistance, which resulted in more health and educational programs as well as expanded agricultural investment. He approved two new laws, Nos. 12 and 19, which established, respectively, government participation in economic development and its ability to fix import quotas. His land reforms were aimed at replacing the family subsistence farm network with a mechanized farming system, bolstered by extended credit and price supports.

While his reformist program temporarily reduced Panama's dependence on canal revenues, it also was a political weapon, emaciating the strength of organized labor, one of his main opposition forces. He also introduced substantive changes to the regressive tax base, enforced tax collection, which had been previously avoided for the most part by the oligarchy, and enacted Panama's first legislation against racial discrimination. In 1952, he signed legislation to open the Colón Free Trade Zone (CFTZ), located at the northern end of the Canal Zone. The CFTZ consisted of warehouses and light factories and would eventually cover 1,600 hectares to become the world's second-largest free trade zone, after Hong Kong. By 1982, the CFTZ would represent over 10 percent of Panama's gross domestic product.[3]

But Remón also had his darker side. He was deeply involved in drug smuggling and a host of other lurid financial activities, such as being part-owner of a house of prostitution, authorizing city bus routes, and selling gasoline to his own police force. To this end, Remón used the National Guard as the repressive agent to guarantee continued rule much as the oligarchy had before him. To ensure loyalty, he authorized benefits to the Guard like medical care, disability pensions, and higher salaries.

One year after taking office, Remón carried out two important political reforms to solidify his power. First, Remón reduced his possible future political opposition by instituting a law called Ley de 45,000 (Law of 45,000), which required that there be 45,000 registered followers before a party would be officially recognized. This high threshold, given the fractured nature of isthmian political parties, left Remón with only the weakened Partido Liberal Nacional to oppose him. This set the foundation for an essentially one-party, military-oriented system that became the model for the later military government that would dominate Panamanian politics.

Second, he bolstered his nationalist credentials by requesting a renegotiation with the United States of the 1903 and 1936 treaties. Remón specifically sought a change in the payment structure from the $430,000 annuity to 20 percent of the canal's annual revenues. Though U.S. President Eisenhower, who had served three years during his military career in the Canal Zone, was sympathetic to Remón's demands, U.S. Secretary of State John Foster Dulles, by contrast, was adamantly against any provision that would reduce the de facto sovereignty of the United States in the Canal Zone.

For Dulles and many in the U.S. intelligence community, the threat of communism loomed large in the world. A contemporary CIA report warned that Latin America was "becoming unglued" because of the growing communist influence behind the scenes. The expropriation that same year in Guatemala of large unused tracts of United Fruit Company's banana holdings together with Egypt's calls to nationalize the Suez Canal seemed to confirm the growing communist threat in Latin America and abroad. But Remón's motto, "Neither alms nor millions, we want justice," which today is inscribed on the facade of the National Assembly in Panama City, inspired Panamanians to strengthen their resolve. Armed with an extensive list of demands that included not only more money from canal operations but the flying of Panama's flag in the Canal Zone, Remón and his negotiators met over the course of a year with U.S. representatives to try to strike a deal. In the end, the United States partially relented to avoid a crisis on the scale of Guatemala or Egypt.

But the Zonians resisted any notion of change. They opposed the new treaty, fearing it would burst the bubble of their utopian existence. Nonetheless, assured that U.S. sovereignty over the canal was not threatened, the U.S. Senate ratified the treaty in 1955. The agreement gave five concessions to Panama: First, it increased Panama's annuity to almost $2 million. But, taking 41 years of inflation into account, the amount was actually less than the original fee the United States paid in 1914.[4] Second, the Canal Zone commissaries' economic advantage was to be restricted, and both U.S. and Panamanian canal employees were to do "as much business as feasible" with Panamanian businesses. More products for the Canal Zone were bought from Panama, and this trade started to contribute significantly to the economy, though canal managers still persisted in purchasing some goods from as far away as Australia. Canal-related economic value for Panama would increase over 700 percent, from $44 million in the 1950s to $343 million by 1979. Third, the United States agreed to construct a bridge near the town of Balboa on the Pacific side that would link the two sides of Panama and provide an important connection for the Pan-American Highway. Completed in 1962, Panamanians dubbed it the "Bridge of the Americas." Fourth, Panama earned the right to tax Panamanian employees in the Canal Zone and gained other concessions such as highway construction, which had previously been the sole purview of the United States.

Last, the United States promised to put Panamanian canal workers' wages on parity with North Americans, though it would take three more years to be implemented. Once in effect, it created a seeming economic boon, since it created the highest hourly wages in all of Latin America.[5] However, an unintended consequence of the high pay was to make Panama a less attractive place for foreign investment, and the Panamanian government could do nothing to ameliorate the situation. The value of the Panamanian balboa was linked by a 1904 monetary treaty to the U.S. dollar, and Panama had become the most wage-expensive country in all of Latin America. Not lost on Panamanians was the fact that the treaty did not address the question of sovereignty over the canal or the dozen U.S. bases that peppered the Canal Zone.

Remón, however, did not live long enough to witness the treaty's implementation nor its outcome. While attending horse races in the countryside on January 2, 1955, he was shot by machine gun, purportedly on orders from the infamous American mobster, "Lucky" Luciano, who wanted to take over Panama's lucrative drug trade. Remón died an hour later at Santo Tomás Hospital. Though the assassins were caught, only one, Rubén Miró, nephew of Harmodio Arias, was brought to trial. He was later acquitted.[6] First Vice President José Ramón Guizado was impeached by the National Assembly, jailed without due process on suspicion of being implicated in the assassination, and then later released, fueling suspicion that there was a conspiracy.

Most of Remón's social reforms died with him, and the oligarchy soon was back in its familiar, though weakened, role as power broker. The winner of the 1956 elections was the CPN's candidate, Ernesto de la Guardia. A more conservative member of the oligarchy, he relaxed the Law of 45,000 to 5,000, effectively diffusing power among political parties and dissolving the previously cohesive CPN bloc, which had been brought together not so much out of ideological unity, but due to the practical necessity of the strength required to overcome the opposition. Once the CPN had lost its guiding principles, several factions split off to form other parties that would run in the 1960 elections.

Panama's relations with the United States steadily worsened. In 1956, at a conference in London held among the world's greatest shipping nations to discuss Egypt's nationalization of the Suez Canal, U.S. Secretary of State Dulles declared that the United States would represent Panama's interests because the United States had "rights of sovereignty" over the Panama Canal. Indignant at the patronizing statement and at not having been invited, as the home of the world's sixth-largest shipping fleet, Panama's government issued a fiery public retort that the United States did not speak for Panama. This proclamation was tantamount to Panamanian diplomatic defiance of the U.S. hegemonic role in the isthmus.

THE ISTHMUS STARTS TO SMOLDER

The Suez conference incident was the match that lit the fuse in the isthmus. After Egypt's nationalization of the Suez Canal, a growing chorus of Panamanians called for even more pay equity and recognition of greater Panamanian sovereignty. De la Guardia's foreign minister, Aquilino Boyd, proposed to Washington that canal revenues be equally shared and that there be a final implementation of pay equity. He was ignored, and the reaction in Panama was stridently nationalistic.

In May 1958 a group of Panamanian students entered the Canal Zone to set up Panamanian flags in "Operation Sovereignty." It was supposed to be a peaceful demonstration of determination, but it quickly deteriorated into bedlam when the National Guard, supported by U.S. soldiers, attacked, wounding 120 students and killing one. The previous ill will between the Panamanian military and the students turned into palpable hostility. This incident prompted President Eisenhower to send his brother, Milton, to investigate the situation. Upon his return to Washington, Milton Eisenhower recommended full implementation of the 1955 treaty, but the Pentagon firmly resisted any modification that might signal a weakening of U.S. resolve regarding the sovereignty question. Again, events outside Panama helped turn the tide.

If the triumph of Fidel Castro's revolution in Cuba in January 1959 sent tremors through Washington, it was a reinvigorating wind for Panamanians railing against U.S. dominance. Castro's overthrow of a U.S.-supported dictatorship gave renewed hope in Panama of forcing the United States to relent on the sovereignty issue. The U.S. presence in the Canal Zone, which divided Panama in two, and the U.S. hegemonic dominance over the country's economy were too similar to Cuba's situation for the United States to discount. The Cuban Revolution stimulated disillusionment within Panamanian society with status quo, and militancy grew ever bolder and louder, with anti-U.S. demonstrations and three ill-planned and poorly equipped insurrections in 1959, one with Cuban assistance.

On November 3, 1959, spurred by provocative articles in newspapers owned by Harmodio Arias, Panamanian students again entered the Canal Zone to plant Panamanian flags for the country's independence day, and were again repelled by U.S. Canal Zone police and Panamanian National Guard units. In the ensuing riot, many buildings were burned and the U.S. ambassador's residence was vandalized. Later the same month, more riots erupted, resulting in 18 deaths.

In response, the Zonians boycotted Panamanian merchants and the United States erected a two-meter-high fence at the entrance to the Zone. Openly stating that he wished to avoid a repeat of the Suez Canal nationalization, President Eisenhower finally agreed to fly the Panamanian flag at Shaler Triangle, a spacious plaza situated near the Panama City end of the Canal Zone, and to implement a host of programs previously suggested by his brother, Milton. Called Operación Amistad (Operation Friendship), the programs were intended to mollify angry Panamanians. Among the changes were a 10 percent raise for Canal Zone workers, the construction of low-cost housing, and the opening of higher-level positions to Panamanians. Most important, Eisenhower suggested for the first time that Panama have some display of "titular sovereignty" in the Canal Zone. However, it was a case of too little, too late. Panamanians were not going to be content with symbolism; they were now demanding tangible, if not sweeping, change.

DISINTEGRATION AMID PROGRESS

As Robert Pastor has noted regarding U.S.-Latin America relations, the United States frequently only increases financial assistance when a crisis is imminent, then quickly cuts the aid once the problem is resolved.[7] Such a moment arrived with the passage in 1961 of President Kennedy's Alliance for Progress program. Created out of the assumption that Castro's revolution and persistent poverty made communism more appealing to Latin America's poor masses, the program, whose principle goal was to sway others from following Castro's example, promised $100 billion in U.S. aid over a decade to Latin American countries.

For Panama, the Alliance for Progress (AFP) brought some tangible economic gains. For the 10-year period from 1951 to 1961, total U.S. economic aid to Panama had been only $7 million. But under the AFP, it increased almost six-fold, to $41 million between 1961 and 1963. Direct military aid to the National Guard increased by an additional $1 million to counter a possible communist threat to the isthmus and the canal. These funds, according to Kennedy's secretary of defense, Robert McNamara, were to help ensure a stable partner against communism that was "capable of maintaining international security against threats of violence and subversion" and encouraging closer civilian and military cooperation. But given Panama's domestic political climate of disdain between the Guard and certain civilian sectors, especially students, the assistance had the opposite effect of only polarizing Panamanian society even more. To further soothe Panamanian sensitivities, Kennedy added 16 more sites within the Zone where the Panamanian flag would fly.

But Panamanians' aggravation was compounded by the establishment under the AFP of the School of the Americas (SOA) in the Canal Zone in 1963. Originally set up in 1946 as the Latin American Training Center, the SOA was redesigned as a center for specialized anti-communist training for Latin American military officers, particularly from Central American armies. The SOA became a centerpiece of U.S. foreign policy in Panama that trained many of the region's future dictators and human-rights abusers, including some from Panama itself.

On March 1, 1960, Panama's Constitution Day, various groups threatened another march into the Canal Zone. The uprisings of the previous year had been sobering for the political elite, who seriously feared that new rioting might become a revolutionary movement against the social system itself. Both of the main coalitions contesting the coming elections sought to avoid further difficulties, and influential merchants, who had been hard hit by the previous riots, were apprehensive. Reports that the United States was willing to recommend flying the republic's flag in a special site in the Canal Zone reduced tensions. The United States agreed to small compromises including submitting taxes from Panamanian canal employees to Panama's government and giving Panamanian employees the same degree of fringe benefits that U.S. employees enjoyed. Nonetheless, many larger issues remained up in the air, such as wage parity between Panamanians and American canal workers.

The 1960 presidential election was most unusual for Panama as it was without major incident and, for the first time in years, the National Guard was largely absent and not the target of accusations of intervention. De la Guardia's administration had been beleaguered by violence and other pressing social and economic problems. The CPN, the loose coalition Remón had hastily assembled, lacked real opposition within the National

Assembly, and thus began to fold. Among those CPN dissenters, most joined the National Liberal Party in a larger coalition called the National Opposition Union (UON).

De la Guardia became the first postwar president to finish a full four-year term in office, and his successor, Roberto Chiari, was the first opposition candidate ever elected to the presidency. Chiari astutely recognized Panama for the time bomb that it was. He first wrote President Kennedy in September 1961 and requested increased benefits from the canal's operation. Kennedy agreed to look into the matter and invited Chiari to Washington the following year. In the end, domestic political wrangling in the United States stymied the effort, even though it had Kennedy's approval.

Chiari also warned Panama's oligarchy that, without the enactment of fundamental social and economic reforms to address the country's social challenges, he might be the last president of the oligarchy. However, the National Assembly was unwilling or unable to act upon the president's petitions, as it was becoming increasingly difficult to openly support any program associated with the United States (the source of most foreign aid) due to the increasing pressure created by the Cuban revolution. Though the Alliance for Progress had been a good start at alleviating social and economic ills in the country and, by the end of Chiari's term, had begun to have a limited effect, the program turned out to be too little, too late. The nationalist situation in Panama came to a head in 1964.

THE FLAG INCIDENT

The year 1964 was the crucible in already tense U.S.-Panamanian relations, and the clash again centered around the flying of the Panamanian flag in the Canal Zone. Since 1960, this issue had been seriously complicated by disagreements between the U.S. Department of Defense and the U.S. Department of State. The U.S. military opposed flying the Panamanian flag, arguing that its presence would be seen as an infringement on U.S. sovereignty in the Canal Zone as well as setting a precedent that might bring greater demands from the Panamanians. The U.S. State Department, in contrast, saw the flag proposal as a reasonable concession to Panamanian demands and a way of saving face on the world stage and defusing a potentially volatile situation.

In January 1963, President Kennedy issued an executive order to fly Panama's flag alongside the U.S. flag at all non-military sites in the Canal. Zonians and their main supporter in Washington, U.S. Representative Daniel Flood, were indignant. But before the new policy was carried out,

Kennedy was assassinated in Dallas. The Johnson administration temporarily shelved Kennedy's Canal Zone policies. One month after Kennedy's assassination, Canal Zone Governor Robert J. Fleming Jr. issued a moratorium on flying either flag in the Zone. Infuriated at what they viewed as a symbolic renunciation of U.S. sovereignty, a large number of Zonians raised U.S. flags all over the Canal Zone without the previously mandated companion Panamanian flags. The Zonians' defiance was countered by an October 1963 Molotov cocktail attack on the U.S. embassy in Panama City. Tempers and frustrations in Panama's social volcano were erupting.

Finally, in January 1964 both flags briefly flew side by side at one rather isolated location. At the ceremony, Panama's "titular" sovereignty over the canal was recognized, but the gesture was diminished by President Chiari's refusal to attend the ceremony. He had earlier requested to personally raise Panama's flag, but was denied by U.S. officials. Panamanians remained dissatisfied with their flag's restricted presence at only one location in the Canal Zone. Though Panama's flag was eventually flown at a few more locations, it remained absent at the Canal Zone's prominent Balboa High School, where a group of U.S. students and their parents had removed it.

On January 9, 1964, a group of students from the University of Panama peacefully entered the Panama Canal Zone determined to fly their flag again in front of the high school. They were met at the flagpole by Zonian students, their parents, and Canal Zone police, and a scuffle broke out. Tempers flared, the Panamanians' flag was ripped, and a riot erupted. Canal Zone police lobbed tear gas at the Panamanians and received a barrage of rocks in return. The U.S. police opened fire with live ammunition. Student began to tear down a high chain-link fence separating the U.S. Canal Zone from Panama, which Colombia's ambassador to the Organization of American States had called Panama's "Berlin Wall." Several students were shot, but the crowds continued to grow, by some estimates, to over 30,000.

U.S.-owned businesses in Panama City, such as Sears and Chase Manhattan bank, were set ablaze, and Panamanian snipers took up positions along the Canal Zone. News of the uprising spread to Panama's second-largest city, Colón, where demonstrators likewise entered the Canal Zone and fought U.S. troops. Smaller acts of violence and vandalism against U.S. interests took place in the cities of David, Santiago, and Chitré, and Panamanian workers at U.S. companies, such as United Fruit, walked off the job. Near Panama City, the U.S. Army's 193rd Infantry Brigade was deployed in armored vehicles, and the U.S. embassy received orders to destroy its sensitive documents and to evacuate its personnel. Canal Zone authorities formally requested the assistance of Panama's National Guard, but were refused, since Guard leaders were painfully aware of the friction caused by their support of the United States the previous year. Many National Guardsmen, in fact, sheltered Americans from the rioters' wrath.

When the National Guard did take the streets four days later, it was simply to clear the streets and seek out looters. The fighting continued in spurts for several days. In the end, more than 28 people had died in the violence, including a number of innocent Panamanians and four U.S. soldiers. Hundreds more were wounded, overflowing Panama City's main hospital, Santo Tomás. Both Panamanian and U.S. media tried to portray the other side as having caused all the deaths, but both sides had equally participated in the carnage. Panamanian investigators found over U.S. 600 bullets embedded in Panama's Legislative Palace and half as many in buildings in the Canal Zone. In addition, millions of dollars in damage had been suffered on both sides.

Four days after the riots, after attending a massive funeral for student "martyrs" that drew over 250,000 mourners, President Chiari broke diplomatic relations with the United States, calling the U.S. response "unjustifiable aggression," an assessment shared by the Organization of American States Council, which released a statement declaring that the U.S. troops had utilized a "disproportionate amount of firepower." International reaction from all corners was critical of the United States. Not only did the Communist bloc roundly denounce U.S. action, but so did some of its closest allies, Britain and France. Major newspapers in the United States such as the *Washington Post* and *New York Times* criticized the colonial character of the Canal Zone as "anachronistic."

President Lyndon B. Johnson was stunned at both the events and the reaction around the world. He assumed that Chiari was using the incident to finally force a new canal treaty. Secretary of the Army Cyrus Vance blamed the riot on Cuban-trained communist agents and claimed that the Panamanians had arrested 10 such agents. Panama's government and the U.S. Department of Defense refuted the claims. All indications were that Communists were only one of many groups who took to the streets. After the riots, a Catholic memorial rally was attended by over 40,000 mourners, whereas a rival communist commemoration the same day drew only 300 participants.

The violence was a catalyst for both sides. In the United States, the Department of Defense issued a report that acknowledged that the creation of the Canal Zone, which divided Panama physically and socioeconomically, was irreconcilable with the future management of peace.[8] The confrontation had demonstrated that the United States would pay a very high price if it attempted to keep the canal "in perpetuity," as the original treaty stipulated.

Chiari demanded a complete revision of the canal treaty, but Johnson refused to commit himself, declaring only that the United States would conduct a "full and frank" review of all canal-related issues. Johnson was careful not to give the impression that the riots had pressured his decision to negotiate. However, after three months of delays, mixed signals, and continued resistance with the U.S. State Department, the United States did begin to discuss a new treaty, and President Johnson announced that plans for a new canal and new treaty would be hammered out in the future.

For Panama, the riots unified a socioeconomically diverse cross-section of Panamanians against the continued U.S. domination of the canal, but also revealed the growing fissures within society. By the 1960s, while a few areas of Panamanian society had improved (for example, literacy had risen to a respectable 77 percent), Panama had one of most unequal income distribution patterns in Latin America. It experienced morbid wage growth and saw increased land concentration by the oligarchy, who wore their legitimacy like a fig leaf. Moreover, the dominance of the canal-related economic activities drew an ever-larger percentage of the population toward the Canal Zone region, further exacerbating housing shortages.[9] Only the continued popular outrage toward the United States protected the oligarchy and its outdated system. The riots had been sobering for the oligarchy, who feared that a new round of riots might upend the system.

The 1964 elections contributed more to the growing unease in the political climate. Though united for sovereignty over the Canal Zone, Panama's political parties were very fragmented in the upcoming 1964 presidential elections. Twenty-two political parties were registered and, between them, supported seven candidates, though only three were considered contenders. Once again, Arnulfo Arias was on the ticket fronting the only party with a mass base, the renovated, nationalist Partido Panameñista (Panamanian Party). He also rediscovered his panache for insulting other sectors of society, this time claiming publicly that all the Panamanians killed in the riots were thugs who "got what they deserved." This rhetoric fit well into his new image as a "friend of the United States." He persisted in ridiculing the oligarchy in order to guarantee massive working-class support.

His principal opposition was Marcos Aurelio Robles, who had served as a minister in Chiari's cabinet. Arias lost the election to Robles amid allegations of fraud to opposition coalitions that had cultivated a hard-line stance toward the United States. Nonetheless, all indications were that Robles defeated Arias legally, thus handing Arias his only legitimate loss at the polls.

For the next three years, treaty talks ebbed and flowed. Further canal treaty discussions took place, but opposition in the United States continued. These concerns spanned the spectrum from the U.S. Pentagon's strategic worries to conservative members of Congress, such as Daniel Flood (labeled by some Panamanians as an "enemy of the Republic"), blamed the whole affair on communist-inspired plans. In 1967 Johnson presented Robles with a draft of a new canal agreement. The proposed agreement was to grant Panama compensation changes regarding the present canal, to create of a nine-member board of governors for the canal, to build a possible sea-level canal, and for a host of military-related matters. In addition, a deadline for turnover in 1999 was proposed. Of additional importance was that all symbols of U.S. hegemony were to be removed from the Canal Zone.

Most of all, it was hoped in both Washington and Panama City that these changes would reduce domestic tensions in Panama, which had reached visible crescendo with protesters camped outside the presidential palace in Panama City. Robles privately agreed that he would not demand a complete revision of the treaty, but was criticized by Panama's National Assembly, which opposed the fact that the United States would still maintain major control of Canal Zone. When drafts of three proposed treaties were made public in 1967, public reaction in Panama was lukewarm at best. Panamanian politicians were not confident about their ability to "sell" these compromises to a very nationalistic Panamanian public, particularly the proposed new board of governors, since Panamanians were to hold only a minority share of the nine seats.

But before the treaties could be properly presented to either the U.S. or Panamanian legislatures, the details were leaked, promoting rancor on both sides, though more on the Panamanian side. The National Assembly's furor ran so high that began impeachment proceedings against Robles, who kept a tenuous hold on power only by virtue of National Guard support. Robles appealed to Panama's Supreme Court, which annulled the impeachment, saying that the National Assembly had "violated" the president's rights, since the Panamanian constitution did not give the National Assembly oversight of a president's performance.

Omnipresent through the proceedings was Brigadier General Bolívar Vallarino, who backed Robles. The message was clear to the National Assembly and the Court—the military did not support the ouster of the president at this time. The National Guard raided the opposition party's headquarters and arrested about 500 people. With the elections in 1968 on the horizon, President Robles forestalled further treaty negotiations until after the elections. His hand-picked PLN successor, David Samudio, was losing the support of the oligarchy, who were rebelling against a plan by Robles to enforce tax collection for the first time on two of Panama's major non-canal sectors, sugar and cement. However, all the effort and acrimony were made pointless by the elections.

In many ways, the elections of 1968 elucidate the strong division between the oligarchs, whose livelihood depended upon the traditional sector of international trade, and the growing lower and middle classes, who were at the forefront of a social movement advocating a shift away from "traditional" politics and exclusionary economics. Arnulfo Arias announced his candidacy once again for president in an extremely divided field where even some members of the oligarchy, such as former President Chiari, lined up in support of Arias.

Opposing him was David Samudio of the Partido Nacional Liberal (Liberal National Party, or PLN). The PLN, a coalition of five minor parties, was created out of the resultant friction within the National Patriotic Coalition (CPN) following the 1960 elections. On the other side, Arias again fronted the nationalist Partido Panameñista. Ever the political manipulator, Arias seemingly renounced his anti-*yanqui* nationalist rhetoric and expressed pro-U.S. sentiments regarding the canal, which made him favorable to Washington. Robles's decision to begin trade with communist nations blacklisted by the United States—China, Cuba, and North Vietnam—did not help matters and drove a wedge between the oligarchy and the U.S. government.

The same old attempt was made by the oligarchy to commit vote fraud, but in the final tally support for Arias was too great to make disappear. Arias was elected president as the candidate of a five-party coalition. Back to his ultranationalist stance, Arias's election ended negotiations for a new treaty. As a person who could never leave well enough alone, he took his election victory as a license for revenge. After he took office on October 1, 1968, Arias began to plan a purge of those National Guard officers who had ousted him previously.

Up to this point in Panama's history, the armed forces had been only a political moderating force, never a direct governing force. Although Arias had not been supported by the National Guard in the election, he was popular among the lower classes from which many Guardsmen now came. Arias planned to assign some key officers to distant sectors of the country or abroad. Among these targeted were Maj. Omar Torrijos, Comm. Bolívar Vallarino, and Sec. Comm. José María Pinilla, who retired rather than succumb to Arias's plan. In their place, Arias planned to install political cronies to solidify his hold on power. Panama's young and fragile democracy was cast aside.

Arias's plan to dispose of these officers humiliated them. They and their fellow officers no long thought of themselves as mere policemen but as a professional military. One publication that had covered the 1968 elections said that "more immediately dangerous to political stability is the ever-present force of nationalism, which has been effectively manipulated by the traditional elite in the past but which now threatens to get out of control." Only 11 days into his presidency, Arias was overthrown by National Guard. For the next 22 years, Panama was to endure a societal upheaval unlike anything in its previous history.

NOTES

1. Michael L. Conniff, *Black Labor on a White Canal* (Pittsburgh: University of Pittsburgh Press, 1985), 116.

2. Michael L. Conniff, *Panama and the United States: The Forced Alliance* (Athens: University of Georgia Press, 1992), 104.

3. Andrew Zimbalist and John Weeks, *Panama at the Crossroads* (Berkeley: University of California Press, 1991), 67.

4. Walter LaFeber, *The Panama Canal: The Crisis in Historical Perspective*, updated ed. (New York: Oxford University Press, 1989), 93.

5. Zimbalist and Weeks, 43.

6. Larry LaRae Pippin, *The Remón Era: An Analysis of a Decade of Events in Panama, 1947–57* (Stanford, CA: Institute of Hispanic American and Luso-Brazilian Studies, 1964), 127–135.

7. Robert A. Pastor, *Whirlpool: U.S. Foreign Policy toward Latin America and the Caribbean* (Princeton, NJ: Princeton University Press, 1992), 21.

8. U.S. Department of Defense, *For Commanders: This Changing World*, Office of Armed Forces Information and Education, January 24, 1964, 4.

9. Zimbalist and Weeks, 30.

5

Dictatorship, Nationalism, and the Canal Treaties, 1968–1981

In 1968, Panama stood fragmented along multiple cleavages. Panama's middle classes had become highly literate and politically active and aware. A growing chorus of nationalism coincided with the recognition that the country's corrupt civilian government, which was typically headed by the *rabiblanco* elite in a strongly entrenched clan power-sharing arrangement, was unfit to solve the country's problems. But, nonetheless, because wealth was still a prerequisite to power, given the funds needed for payoffs in the country's corrupt political system, being part of the elite was still perceived as the best route to office. The party system that existed prior to 1968 served only to regulate political competition among the oligarchy, and individual parties typically were just the personal political vehicles of leaders. Clientelism, the bestowing of jobs or other advantages to supporters, was rampant, as was graft.

Fronting his own party, the nationalist Partido Panameñista (PP), Arnulfo Arias's election to his third presidential victory in 1968 piqued a macabre interest in both Panama and Washington. For 18 tension-filled days Panama's Election Tribunal—beholden to the elites—had sought a way to overturn Arias's win but, in the end, the National Guard's commander, Bolívar Vallarino, relented in supporting his former nemesis, since it would have been very difficult to make Aria's 50,000 winning vote margin disappear. Washington had come to appreciate Arias's apparently new cooperative and conciliatory stance toward the United States, which fit well within the U.S. foreign policy in Latin America of "stability-first, democracy-second," especially regarding the Panama Canal.

But Arias was not content with mere victory; he wanted total control. Once in office, he eschewed his pro-U.S. stance and demanded that Panama be given immediate jurisdiction over the Canal Zone. Arias then planned to make the National Guard less of a danger by firing its two most senior officers, Vallarino and Colonel José María Pinilla, and appointing the more loyal Colonel Bolívar Urrutia to command the force. While he did convince Vallarino to resign his Guard leadership for a plush position in Panama's embassy in Washington, his power-shifting machinations guaranteed he would again not complete a term as president.

Though not all the National Guard officers favored military rule, they were united that Arias not be allowed to carry out his plan. On October 11, 1968, Panama's National Guard toppled Arias for the third time. In a near-bloodless coup, Arias loyalists were arrested and, having been forewarned, Arias himself as well as most of his ministers and 24 National Assembly members fled into the Canal Zone. Arias's pleas for U.S. intervention were unheeded. Though U.S. Secretary of State Dean Rusk ordered diplomatic relations with Panama suspended for a month, the fact that at the time the majority of Latin American countries was under or was falling to military dictatorship meant that the United States finally recognized the new military regime. This decision was eased by the understanding that the National Guard was a constant force to curtail student protests, and the university students were perceived to be one of the greatest potential obstacles to the 1967 draft treaties. In addition, the new Nixon administration also viewed the anticipated postponement of a new canal treaty during the period of the National Guard's consolidation of power to be beneficial, since the United States was itself convulsing in domestic conflict over the Vietnam War and civil rights protests.

Immediately following the coup, there were the anticipated student protests as well as sporadic clashes for several months between the National Guard and peasants in the Province of Chiriquí. Though initially arrested for his closeness to Arias, Urrutia was later persuaded to join in the two-man provisional junta headed by Pinilla. They headed a ruling council named two days after the coup that included both military and civilian members. The five civilians, including a well-known lawyer, Roberto Alemán, were brought in for their experience and contacts in the U.S. government to assuage the U.S. anxiety over a smooth transition.

Pinilla named himself provisional president and declared that elections were forthcoming. However, by January 1969, Colonel Boris Martínez and Lieutenant Colonel Omar Torrijos had risen from within ranks to hold the real power. Though some accounts portray Torrijos as the coup leader, he was reportedly at first a reluctant participant, having been forced into action at the point of a gun.[1] But once ensconced in the leadership, Torrijos took advantage of his newfound power.

The civilians in the government lasted only three months. They resigned en masse, accusing the National Guard of dictatorial practices, which included the disbandment of the National Assembly, the closure of the University of Panama for several months, the criminalization of opposition political parties and the ransacking of their offices, and in a few cases, the exile of prominent businessmen.

Seeking to assure the United States about Panama's new direction, Torrijos met soon after the coup with Canal Zone Commander General Chester Johnson to discuss the new government. However, suspecting that the U.S. military might try to reinstall Arias, Torrijos fled during a coffee break, almost provoking a shoot-out with U.S. soldiers while exiting the zone. Torrijos later threatened to "burn the Canal Zone" if an attempt to reinstall Arias were made.[2] Since the U.S. military itself had recognized the canal's vulnerability to domestic attack along a perimeter extending over 200 kilometers, the threat was taken seriously.[3] By the end of the year, the coup was a fait accompli.

Only a few months later, in March 1969, Martínez was ousted from the power-sharing arrangement. On national television, he had promised a series of radical land and business reforms and tacit support of anti-American protests that had spooked the oligarchy. This provoked a countercoup that was led by Torrijos and encouraged by the United States. Torrijos did not denounce the proposed reforms, but he was careful not to antagonize Panamanian and United States investors, ensuring them that their financial interests were not threatened. Martínez and three other officers were sent into exile in Miami. Torrijos promoted himself to the rank of brigadier general and assumed dictatorial powers, but retained Pinilla as the ceremonial president.

ENIGMATIC DICTATORSHIP

Omar Torrijos Herrera was arguably the most enigmatic of Latin America's modern dictators. The son of a school teacher of modest means from the western Panama province of Veraguas, as a youth Torrijos absorbed ideals of social justice and fervent nationalism. He attended and graduated from El Salvador's military academy on a scholarship, and then received specialized training at the U.S. military's School of the Americas (SOA) in the Canal Zone, which became infamous for using training manuals for Latin American officers that advocated execution, torture, blackmail, and other forms of coercion against Latin American insurgents and members of the political left (as admitted to by the U.S. Department of Defense in 1996). At the SOA Torrijos was recruited as a part-time spy by the U.S. Central Intelligence Agency, a relationship that lasted until his dictatorship began.[4] He had been promoted through the ranks by Remón, with whom he shared a sense of mission to national sovereignty. It was during these years that Torrijos distinguished himself in both quelling and sympathizing with social unrest. He expressed doubts about the elites' ability to deal with the growing discontent.

Never before had modern Panama endured a military dictatorship, and Torrijos was unique both as Panama's first military strongman and as the first Latin American leader since Fidel Castro to stand resolutely against the U.S. hegemony in Latin America. Torrijos lived in two worlds simultaneously: On one hand, he looked and sometimes acted the part of the stereotypical Latin American *caudillo,* but on the other, he frequently would reveal an irreverent, and even staunch, Panamanian nationalism against the U.S. presence and influence.[5] .

One telling anecdote describes Torrijos receiving a diplomatic note relayed from the U.S. Congress by the U.S. ambassador to Panama, Ambler Moss, Jr., which demanded certain concessions regarding Panama's assistance of El Salvador's guerrillas. The general returned the message with a hand-written note saying, "I don't accept this message since it was sent to the wrong address. It should have been sent to Puerto Rico."[6] Thus, in addition to wit and sarcasm, one of Torrijos's most renowned attributes was his profound sense of pragmatism rather than romanticism. This pragmatism, coupled with strong nationalism, is demonstrated by his declaration about his ultimate goal: "I do not want to enter into history. I want to enter into the Canal Zone."

For the first time since the 1959 Cuban revolution, U.S. hegemony in the Caribbean basin was challenged. Torrijos's legitimacy among Panamanians gave him considerable leverage at home and against Washington. Torrijos's conception of Panama's political climate contained an innate understanding that his rule would depend on the involvement of the popular groups that traditionally had not benefited from Panama's oligarchic rule, such as the lower classes, laborers, and student groups. Adroitness would be needed to restructure Panama's relationship with the United

States if Panama hoped to gain control of the canal. To solidify his domestic support, Torrijos made an alliance with Panama's Communist Party, the Partido Popular, which had consistently opposed Arias and the U.S. presence. But he also imprisoned (or worse) those members who would not toe the line.

The rule of Torrijos was seriously challenged only once. In December 1969, while attending horse races in Mexico City with a long-time friend, Demetrio Basilio Lakas, Torrijos received an urgent message to call Panama. Torrijos was told by three National Guard officers, Amado Sanjur, Luís Nentzen Franco, and Ramiro Silvera, that he had been overthrown. With money borrowed from a young employee at Panama's embassy in Mexico, Torrijos and Lakas rented an air-taxi and rushed back to Panama, making a dangerous nighttime landing in the city of David.[7] Once at National Guard headquarters in Panama City, Torrijos found the conspirators already under arrest by loyal officers. Only Torrijos's intervention spared their lives.

Torrijos deposed Pinilla as president for not having opposed the coup attempt and replaced him with Lakas as a reward for the latter's loyalty and to promote some semblance of order. Lakas, however, was simply a symbolic president, since all decision making now rested with Torrijos. Nonetheless, Torrijos astutely realized that Panama still had to exist in a divided financial and political world. To appeal to both international bankers and to leftists alike, he surrounded himself with advisers and ministers from across the political and intellectual spectrum as well as Panama's diverse socioethnic divisions of the *pueblo* (common people, mostly mestizo) and *rabiblancos*. His pragmatism meant that Torrijos was equally comfortable with elitists and leftists, so long as there was an advantage to be had.

The United States tried to convince Torrijos to follow in the more moderate pattern of other Latin American military dictatorships of the time that were largely amiable to U.S. policy in the region. But Torrijos was not interested, and even went out of his way to contravene U.S. wishes, developing friendships with such implacable U.S. enemies as Cuba's Fidel Castro and Libya's Momar Qadhafi.

He was equally persistent that there be a Panamanian solution to the country's social problems, not just more U.S. aid with conditions. In his typical penetrating folk wisdom, Torrijos was fond of saying, "a Panamanian does not put on an overcoat when it is snowing in Washington; we seek our own solutions." Nonetheless, Torrijos was keenly aware of the geopolitical reality of the U.S. presence in his country, and never pushed too hard in the early years to embarrass the United States. Throwing out an occasional anti-U.S. barb for domestic consumption, though, was par for the course.

REFORMS AND CONSOLIDATION

Panama's oligarchy had typically ignored Panama's population outside the Canal Zone region. As a mercantile oligarchy, it had been strongly tied to both American business interests and the benefits of the Canal Zone. This relationship explains the oligarchy's non-nationalistic stance, since the United States provided the best-paying jobs to Panamanians, releasing the oligarchy from the responsibility of providing a more equitable society. But while the United States provided a sizable portion of the good jobs, it also created a situation in which the oligarchy's close relationship to U.S. interests had lost it much legitimacy with Panama's population.

Torrijos considered the issue of the Panama Canal's ownership to be the best leverage against the United States. But since the United States continued to balk at true canal negotiations, Torrijos used the U.S. foot dragging to declare a moratorium on further talks while he got his domestic house in order. The United States countered by commissioning feasibility studies with Colombia for a new, sea-level canal to put additional pressure on the Panamanians to accept a lesser settlement. This ploy, however, was seen through by Panama's delegation, since the cost for a new sea-level canal would have been prohibitively high at about $20 billion.[8]

During the first few years of his rule, Torrijos mounted a steady campaign to consolidate power and to dampen U.S. hegemony in the country. He declared that his reform package was part of a *revolución*, a term that perked up ears in Washington. Similar to what other Latin American populists of the time had done upon seizing power, Torrijos nationalized a few smaller U.S.-owned companies. But in one case, the Power and Light Company, Panama purchased the entity so as to not stir up too much ire from Washington. Nonetheless, foremost on Torrijos's agenda were reforms involving sweeping representational changes in the government, agricultural reform, rapid economic growth, and a redefinition of labor relations.

To ensure the changes, Torrijos utilized the classic Latin American approach of *pan o palo* (bread or stick). The *pan* was his promotion of a leftist, populist agenda that reduced the power of the oligarchy and improved the lot of many poor Panamanians. Of Panama's 1.5 million people in 1968, 38 percent lived in poverty, 13 percent were illiterate, and 10 percent of its children were malnourished. In addition, 50,000 subsistence farmers eked out a living on less than $100 annually. These indicators were comparatively better than in other Central American countries, a situation that had allowed Panama's oligarchy a certain amount of freedom from overt concern for the poor, since the United States had supported or implemented public works projects in and around the Canal Zone. But the extent of outright poverty, especially when compared to the living standards in the Canal Zone, gave Torrijos a reason to make social justice the top priority of his new government's agenda. Such populism ensured the support of the poor.

With the export sector expanding at 10 percent annually, the economy that Torrijos inherited was on very sound footing, which initially assisted him in his reformist ambitions. However, government income derived from taxes never deviated from 15 percent of GNP, while Torrijos's government spending skyrocketed. Social programs grew over 700 percent, resulting in some impressive results: Infant mortality dropped by 40 percent; the number of public schools increased by 50 percent; literacy, already the highest in Central America, increased by 20 percent; and social security was expanded to cover 60 percent of the population compared to just 12 percent before his rule. An extensive cabinet reorganization, including members of Panama's communist party, and the comments by Torrijos and other high-ranking officials in 1971, heralded the shift in domestic policy. Torrijos expressed admiration for the socialist trends in the leftist military governments of Bolivia and Peru, but he was still careful to publicly distance himself from Panama's communists.

The year 1972 was central to setting Panama's new direction. For the first four years, Torrijos had ruled by fiat, and elections promised early on by the military had never come to fruition. Instead of elections, Torrijos promised the oxymoronic-sounding "democracy without elections." In March 1972, he announced the formation of a Constitutional Reform Commission to revise the 1946 constitution and move representational power away from the oligarchy. The constitution that emerged, though democratic in some aspects and language, was radically different in both form and practice from Panama's previous constitution.

The new constitution was presented in 1972 to the new legislative body, called the National Assembly of Corregimientos. *Corregimientos* were essentially extremely small counties (there were 505 in the country) whose allocation of seats was disproportionately tilted toward the previously neglected rural areas. Torrijos understood that outside of the Canal Zone, where almost half the population resided, Panama was still an agricultural country. In the peasants lay the root of the power that gave Torrijos a large base capable of keeping the oligarchy in check.

As a result of the reorganization, rural areas received disproportionally large amounts of long-overdue public works projects, such as health clinics, hospitals, and infrastructure. To further influence rural opinion of the regime, over 130 *asentamientos* (rural cooperatives) were established, redistributing land to the landless. Though Panama's economy depended a great deal on the canal and its related service sector, the country's agricultural sector was still economically important. However, an increasing share of arable land was either corporate-owned, particularly by the United Fruit Company, or part of immense landed estates. Each *corregimiento* sent a representative to the Assembly once a year, and these representatives were given a venue for voicing their opinions to the national government, while Torrijos was afforded a direct link to every corner of the country for imposing the regime's will.

The Assembly was further subdivided into a National Assembly of Representatives and the National Council of Legislation, both of which were essentially powerless. Decisions continued to emanate from Torrijos. Aside from the façade of governmental structure, the most significant changes were provisions that allowed the Panamanian president to delegate his authority to another person or entity, and the president was given no authority over the National Guard. Since Torrijos still controlled decision making, these "stipulations" were insurance against a puppet president becoming too ambitious.

This provision also made the National Guard an officially autonomous actor, free from civilian oversight, which suited Torrijos, since the new constitution additionally gave him six more years of dictatorial rule under the title "Maximum Leader of the Panamanian Revolution" to make "revolutionary" changes. For good measure, the new constitution also empowered the government to "protect the purity of the Spanish language," which was one of many jabs the Torrijos regime made at the U.S. presence in Panama.

To consolidate support among the working classes, Torrijos promulgated a key populist reform the same year called, appropriately enough, the *Labor Code*. The legislation was meant to soften the criticism the Torrijos regime had drawn in its early years for not holding elections as promised. Backed by a strong Ministry of Labor, the legislation radically shifted the balance of negotiating power toward labor, which, along with peasants, composed a significant proportion of Panama's population. The labor code distinguished the Torrijos regime from Panama's less labor-friendly oligarchic past by instituting price freezes, an extra month's bonus pay annually, maternity leave, and compulsory collective bargaining.

Taking a cue from the successful Mexican corporatist approach, the Torrijos government also co-opted labor by making union membership mandatory and creating a "workers' bank" to provide low-cost, income-adjusted loans. From 1973 to 1978, union membership increased from

3,258 to over 58,000, encompassing over 20 percent of Panama's workforce, ranging from factory workers down to street peddlers. In addition, to soothe the nationalist Arnulfistas, legislation was passed to reduce the number of foreign-born workers allowed in the workplace from 25 percent to 10 percent. These reforms, along with numerous other worker- and peasant-oriented changes, solidified popular support for Torrijos and formed the basis for the support for military rule for the next decade and a half.

Torrijos was not without fault, ambition, or inequality. His down-to-earth demeanor was spiced with an ever-present bottle of whiskey, which, according to R. M. Koster and Guillermo Sánchez, symbolized the glut of borrowing and corruption into which Torrijos would lead Panama.[9] Nepotism was rampant during Torrijos's rule, with over 40 members of his extended family serving in high government positions or operating questionable businesses ranging from gambling to prostitution. Torrijos's own brother, Mochi, was infamous for his drug trafficking.

As Panamanian historian Ricaurte Soler points out, Torrijos's reforms were not ultimately comprehensive and, in fact, ended up favoring the development of the services sector and the middle class.[10] Only 4 percent of rural farmers actually benefited from land reforms. While Torrijos did improve the lot of some of the workers and the poor, his most important and lasting reforms concerned the expansion of commerce and the banking sector.

Foreign investment was lured to Panama by the offer of tax incentives and provisions for the unlimited repatriation of capital. In particular, international banking was encouraged to locate in Panama through a 1970 law creating "off-shore" banking. Funds borrowed abroad could be loaned to foreign borrowers without being taxed by Panama. Laws were passed that liberalized banking regulations to include tax exemptions, numbered accounts, and the elimination of reserve minimums, making Panama an extremely attractive financial center, with some of it, undoubtedly, including laundered funds.

Panama became, as it still is, the "Switzerland of Latin American banking." Money, both licit and illicit, flowed in and out of Panama's banks at a prodigious rate and under complete secrecy. Within a decade the number of banks and their total deposits blossomed from 23 banks holding $1 billion to 130 banks with $50 billion in assets. This is a doubly remarkable figure considering the country's average GDP for the same time period was just $3.6 billion.[11] In effect, these banking reforms returned the country to its traditional role as a crossroads of illicit trade. But, ultimately, the growth of banking resulted in what Torrijos was seeking to avoid—the continued dominance of foreign ownership of the economy. By 1976, 91 percent of deposits resided in foreign-owned banks.[12]

The social programs and the liberalization of banking inflicted a high economic cost. The Torrijos regime's statist approach in promotion of the economy meant that within ten years public-sector employment was one-quarter of all jobs in Panama, even though the tax base had not grown to fund the increase. To continue programs, the government borrowed ever-increasing amounts to sustain payrolls and the economy. By 1976, Panama would owe lenders over $1.3 billion, or almost $1,000 per capita in a country where the GDP per capita was only $1,108.

THE STICK

To ensure implementation of and adherence to his reforms, the Torrijos regime employed a *palo* (stick) in the form of an expected increase in the presence of the National Guard in Panamanian life. Since the time of Remón, the National Guard had infiltrated many sectors of society, but under Torrijos, its professionalization, prestige, and benefits were augmented considerably. This, in fact, was the most important reform during Panama's years of dictatorship. Though Remón had attracted more money from the United States for weaponry and had changed the name from the National Police to the National Guard, Torrijos made more important changes that made the Guard a loyal and efficient supporter of his programs, reforms, and the mission to gain the canal.

Two military-related institutions were created. A military academy, the Instituto Militar General Tomás Herrera, was established at the Omar Torrijos Military Base in Río Hato. Modeled on Peruvian military schools, it offered training for those who might some day choose to pursue a military career. Concurrently, the José Domingo Espinar Educational Center was opened, replacing the U.S. Army School of the Americas (SOA) as a source of further training for Panamanian officers. At both institutions, in addition to sine qua non military education, the curriculum was shifted from an emphasis on the Guard's longstanding Cold War role toward one that accentuated social awareness and economic training, such as agronomy and economics.

Outside of the classroom the National Guard was well cared for, which helped ensure its loyalty to the regime. Health care and pensions were universalized for the officer corps, and the Union Club, the oligarchy's stylish getaway, was commandeered and turned into a National Guard recreation center. Civil liberties were limited and state-sponsored censorship of the media was imposed, and civilians who insulted or showed contempt for military officials were dealt with severely in law and punishment. This practice, which had its genesis during Remón's presidency, formed the basis for the law that penalizes public criticism of the government in the media, which is still in force to this day.

To enhance the regime's surveillance capabilities, Torrijos appointed Manuel Noriega as chief of the G-2, Panama's military intelligence agency. Torrijos freely referred to Noriega as "my gangster" because of the latter's penchant for both violence and illicit financial activities. The reach and influence of the G-2 became so great that some Panamanian politicians, even presidents, considered it the functional power that ran the country.[13] Noriega's affinity for blatant cruelty served this post well. As John Dinges aptly notes, the relationship between Torrijos and Noriega was symbiotic— Torrijos handed out bread while Noriega meted out sticks.[14]

But the fear imposed by the Torrijos regime was different than that in other parts of Latin America during the era. If the contemporary military governments of Argentina and Chile used political violence like a sickle, hacking through the political opposition, then Panama's violence was more of a sniper, seeking to impose maximum fear with minimal collateral damage. For example, in 1971, Father Héctor Gallego, a Colombian priest working in Panama, was arrested for conducting *conscientización* (political awareness) activities in his parish and for organizing agricultural cooperatives that threatened the commercial interests of Torrijos's relatives. Under Noriega's supervision, he was thrown in the ocean from a helicopter by members of the G-2 (who were subsequently convicted of the murder in 1993).[15] A later 1977 investigation by a special commission of the International Commission on Human Rights found that at least 34 murders were attributable to the Torrijos regime, most occurring during these early formative years of military rule.

Though the government was most certainly undemocratic, and occasionally brutal, the social changes undertaken by Torrijos were the most sweeping and transforming in Panama's history. But most important, the institutionalization of the dictatorship provided a measure of legitimacy to the Torrijos regime that gave it the time and space necessary to work toward the ultimate goal of gaining control of the Panama Canal.

DAVID AGAINST GOLIATH

Though Torrijos had initially discarded the 1967 draft canal treaties, by 1971 he had tried to restart negotiations. However, this attempt ended in frustration and stalemate because of a lack of official support and the inability to find common ground for compromise. Panama simply wanted more than the United States was willing to give at the time.

When Nixon's administration delayed at further talks, Torrijos's antagonistic streak bubbled to the top, emphasizing his friendship with Washington's enemies, which was interpreted by the United States as a possible prelude to "another Cuba." Torrijos, however, never pushed his antagonism too far, and, ever the pragmatist, even cooperated with the United States on security and economic issues in the Caribbean basin. Assisted by a team of shrewd Panamanian negotiators, Torrijos began to construct a case to garner support in the world community for Panama to control the canal.

Torrijos was determined to gain the canal bearing his country's name, both for economic and nationalist reasons. By the early 1970s, due to price fluctuations and United Fruit Company's domination of fruit production, agricultural exports had become an unreliable source of income. On the other hand, the canal provided a steady stream of income. About 5 percent of world trade transited the canal, amounting to about 30 percent of Panama's foreign trade, 25 percent of its foreign exchange earnings, and 13 percent of its GNP. Though not the only economic enterprise (services were now by far the largest), the canal was still an integral producer for the nation's economy, though Panama received just a little over $2 million of the canal's annual revenues of over $15 million.

In 1972 Panamanian diplomats began an unremitting assault on the United States in the court of world opinion. The central themes of the January 1972 UN Security Council (UNSC) meeting held in Addis Ababa, Ethiopia, were colonialism and racism, which befitted Panama's plans. During the meeting, Panama's UN ambassador, Aquilino Boyd, unleashed a blistering and emotional critique of the U.S. presence in the Canal Zone, highlighting Panama's neocolonial status and warning of the danger of further confrontation between the two countries. Stunned by the unexpected tirade, the U.S. ambassador to the UN, George H. W. Bush, tried to defuse the anger, but Boyd received a rousing round of applause.

By bringing the canal issue before the UN, Panama hoped that it would find sympathy for its situation from the rest of the third world, much of which was in the midst of similar struggles against the vestiges of colonialism. Since these developing countries were now three-fourths of the UN membership, Torrijos had decided to bring the problem out in the open to accelerate U.S. action.

Since Panama held a rotating seat on the UNSC, Boyd, as well as the foreign minister, Juan Antonio Tack, lobbied the UNSC members to hold its next meeting in Panama. The Panamanians anticipated that with such an international forum, world leaders could be convinced of the virtue of Panama's position. Despite U.S. objections, in Resolution 325 the Council called a special meeting in Panama City for the following year. Sensing the weight of the changing tide of Panamanian and world opinion, the U.S. National Security Council (NSC) issued a statement to the Nixon administration that the time had come to change the U.S.-Panama relationship in a substantial way.

The depth of discontent was apparent at the meeting in March 1973, where dignitaries were greeted by a sign outside the conference asking, "What country of the world can bear the humiliation of a foreign flag piercing its heart?" The mood was set. As host, Torrijos gave the introduction, which at such gatherings is usually confined to mere pleasantries. Instead, he unleashed a blistering denouncement of the U.S. presence in Panama and the resistance by the United States to further negotiations. He warned that continued opposition would "force violent change." Moved by this argument, the UNSC issued a resolution (which had been secretly drafted in advance by Panama's Foreign Ministry) that called for the United States to negotiate a "just and equitable" treaty. The gauntlet had been thrown.

But the new U.S. ambassador to the United Nations, John Scali, had been forewarned that Panama might pick a fight. At the direction of the Nixon's national security adviser, Henry Kissinger, the United States employed its veto power to quash the proposal, saying that the Panama Canal was a bilateral issue and not open for discussion in the United Nations. But amid mass support for the measure, the sole veto of the United States became its embarrassment. For Panama, its short-term loss was actually a long-term gain. The issue's dramatization garnered wide international support, particularly among Latin American states, whose mineral wealth the United States coveted amid the Cold War. The Panama Canal was one of the few subjects that galvanized Latin America's usually nationally focused leaders against the United States. Additional firm international pressure finally forced the United States back to the negotiating table.

Some disconcerted elements within the U.S. government wanted Torrijos to go the way of Chile's Salvador Allende, and even hatched a plan to assassinate him.[16] Later in 1973 the United States renewed talks on the picturesque Panamanian island of Contadora. Based on a proposal draft written by Tack, in February 1974, Kissinger signed a version of the so-called "eight principles" for direct negotiations toward, in Kissinger's words, a "just and equitable treaty" that would defuse the ongoing tensions between the two countries. These principles included the recognition of Panama's sovereignty over the Canal Zone, increased payments, and, most importantly, a date for the U.S. turnover of the canal to Panama. But the train of progress ground to a halt later that year, held up by the Watergate scandal and President Nixon's subsequent resignation.

The new U.S. president, Gerald Ford, came into office hoping to heal the emotional wounds of the United States but also to bring the new canal treaty to fruition. Ford promoted the treaty's passage, but negotiations became mired in political retrenchment among U.S. lawmakers over four issues: Panama's percentage of the canal's revenues, the amount of land U.S. military bases would continue to occupy in the Canal Zone, the duration of the treaty, and U.S. demands for new, renewable leases on military bases, which would run for 40 to 50 years. Resistance to changes in the status quo was especially strong among conservative U.S. senators Strom Thurman and Jesse Helms, who along with 38 co-sponsors, put up a sufficient united front to stop passage of any treaty in the U.S. Senate.

These U.S. lawmakers felt that any retreat from absolute sovereignty over the canal would signal weakness to the world. But the principal concern was that any change in the status quo could conceivably weaken the U.S. economic and military posture, and thus their inflexible position on the clause of "in perpetuity" within the original treaty. The pinnacle of U.S. resistance was signaled by a future U.S. president, Ronald Reagan, who used the divisive issue in his campaign for California governor. Based on a briefing secretly received from Arnulfo Arias, Reagan declared that "We built it [the Panama Canal], we paid for it, and we are going to keep it," obviating the fact that Theodore Roosevelt himself had declared that Panama should have sovereignty over the Canal Zone, since no Panamanian ever signed the original treaty.

For this reason and others, Ford had great difficulty building support among U.S. lawmakers. However, resistance was greatest from the Pentagon, which saw its military bases as a non-negotiable point. But public opinion in Panama, goaded by Torrijos, was reaching a crescendo. To put added pressure on Washington toward action on the treaty, Torrijos formally renewed diplomatic ties with Cuba, while, in turn, Cuba exploited Panama's Colón Free Trade Zone to circumvent the U.S. trade embargo against the island. Coupled with Panama's joining the Cuba-formed Non-Aligned Movement, the mere appearance that Panama was moving more to the left reinforced the need on the part of the United States for action, which was what Torrijos had calculated.

But when Kissinger inadvertently stated in public in September 1975 that the United States intended to maintain the indefinite right to defend the canal, Panamanians' patience was exhausted. This intransigent statement incited a group of over 500 enraged Panamanian students to attack the U.S. embassy in Panama City with bricks and rocks, with the regime's tacit approval. The National Guard watched the melee from afar until they themselves were attacked, after which they cleared the streets.

Recognizing that the canal issue was an obstacle to obtaining greater cooperation from other Latin American countries, resistance began to fade in the U.S. Congress. But the canal became a key issue in the 1976 U.S. presidential elections, causing retrenchment by Ford on the issue of U.S. sovereignty in order to capture more votes among conservatives. The Democratic challenger, Jimmy Carter, a former Georgia governor and U.S. Navy officer, understood the strategic value of the middle ground. Carter promised to work toward an equitable solution that would not compromise, but would in fact bolster U.S. security while addressing Panama's demands.

Virtually since its independence, Panama had pressed for changes in the 1903 treaty. But the Panamanian bargaining position was inherently poor, since it had negotiated from a position of weakness, and as such the United States felt no pressing need to pay much attention to Panamanian requests. As former Carter adviser Robert Pastor has noted, it seemed counterintuitive from the U.S. standpoint to assume that giving up control of the canal would protect it.[17] But the resolution of the canal situation was deemed an imperative step toward easing relations with the rest of Latin America.

The Commission on U.S.-Latin American Relations called the renegotiation of the Panama Canal treaties "the most urgent issue the new administration will face in the Western Hemisphere." In addition, the history of bilateral relations between the United States and Panama convinced Carter of the moral righteousness of the new canal treaties. As former U.S. ambassador to Panama William Jordan notes, the need for a new canal treaty was a subject that "was misunderstood by two-thirds of the American people, which converted it into a ready-made target for opportunists and demagogues."[18]

But, incisively, Carter recognized that without compromise, it was likely that the old treaties, unchanged, would endanger the canal far more than Cold War adversaries. Torrijos had issued threats against the canal before and, under sufficient domestic pressure, might be pushed to follow through. In fact, Torrijos and many other Panamanian officials held a deep-seated conviction that the United States would never accede to Panama's demands and that violence would be the only tool left. It was for precisely this reason that Torrijos had established the Cochinos Salvajes

(Wild Pigs), a specialized military unit whose sole purpose was to conduct guerrilla warfare against the Canal Zone.[19]

True to his character, Carter was determined to appeal as much to Panamanians' sense of dignity and economic problems as to U.S. military concerns. By 1976, Panama's economic situation was rapidly deteriorating. Canal revenues were more important than ever to sustain Panama's social welfare state. The waterway remained the country's single most important source of revenue, now generating least 40 percent of GDP. Additionally, the lack of a new canal treaty had begun to undermine Torrijos's popularity. The canal issue had served Torrijos as a natural focal point to focus the population's attention away from domestic problems; now it hung like an albatross around his neck. Rising world oil prices had spurred rampant inflation, driving up the cost of essential foods and producing more unemployment. For the first time since Torrijos took power, protesters were in the streets directing their anger toward his regime, not the United States. A crackdown by the National Guard only exacerbated the situation. Panama's social pot was close to boiling over.

HAMMERING OUT TREATIES

In 1977, Carter asserted, "We will put our relations with Latin America on a more constructive basis, recognizing the global character of the region's problems."[20] While not factoring into his victory, the negotiation of new Panama Canal treaties was the top priority sent by Carter to the U.S. National Security Council after his election. The process was to proceed using the Kissinger-Tack principles, though Panama had swapped Tack with a number of replacements, ending up with Rómulo Escobar Bethancourt as its chief negotiator. The chief negotiators for the United States were the U.S. ambassador to Panama, Ellsworth Bunker, and a corporate lawyer, Sol Linowitz.

For Torrijos, the canal treaty renegotiation took on an even greater importance: a means to sustain his rule. The regime viewed a new treaty as the only salvation for its continued rule. In 1977 Panama teetered on the edge of economic and social collapse. Though the early reforms had bought Torrijos some goodwill among a significant segment of the population, that progress came at a greater cost than Panama could afford. Economic growth had shrunk to less than 2 percent annually and the country was borrowing even more from U.S. banks to sustain public works programs, digging itself deeper into debt. Panama's cities were bursting at the seams with both new migrants from the countryside and a burgeoning youth demographic. These difficulties were not lost on students at the University of Panama, who always had been the country's political bellwether. Instead of the typical anti-U.S. rhetoric and graffiti, the messages found at the university became more critical of the domestic downturn, thus tacitly criticizing the regime. For Torrijos, the writing was literally on the wall.

The difficult situation caused the regime to take two measures, both of which only increased the mounting tensions. First, to rekindle economic growth, development emphasis was shifted from the popular sectors to attracting foreign investment. The leftist reformers who had found a place in the regime were ousted in favor of more business-friendly officers and programs. The labor reforms of 1972 were weakened and land redistribution was rolled back somewhat, with the largest farms increasing holdings and the smallest farms being broken into even smaller, frequently unsustainable, parcels.

TWO-STEP PROCESS

The negotiations began in earnest in 1977. The one persistent obstacle was Panama's objection to the U.S. demand to leave a provision that would allow it to ensure the canal's neutrality for the indefinite future. The Panamanians rightly understood this to mean military intervention, which made the clause a hard sell to Panama's population, which had in their minds endured constant U.S. intervention since 1903. However, U.S. negotiators made it clear that such a provision, while still in the midst of the Cold War, was a sine qua non for approval in the U.S. Senate, which approves all U.S. treaties.

Though hopeful that Carter would prevail against his congressional opponents, Torrijos hedged his bets by continuing to seek support among leftist world leaders who were diametrically opposed to U.S. interests. He met with the Libyan leader Momar Qadhafi to gain his support, established a stronger diplomatic relationship with Cuba, symbolically pledged the Panamanian military to a fight against the brutal Afrikaner regime in South Africa, and signed an economic agreement with the Soviet Union. Additionally, to wring every bit of benefit from a new canal treaty, Torrijos began to make exorbitant demands such as claiming Panama deserved over $1 billion to redress the country for the previous use of the Canal Zone. Though such ranting was meant for Panamanian domestic consumption to satisfy an increasingly anxious population, it had the opposite effect in Washington.

Members throughout the U.S. Congress protested Panama's intransigence, including even Barry Goldwater, who had previously counterbal-

anced conservatives' opposition. Carter soothed their fears, stating that
the treaty would allow the United States the right to "maintain the neutrality" of the canal. This aggravated Panamanian negotiators, who correctly evaluated such a provision as a way to keep some semblance of
sovereignty under the guise of openness.

The treaties were finally signed by President Carter and General Torrijos
on September 7, 1977, in front of representatives of 26 other Western Hemisphere states. The two men could not have been more different in character
and temperament, but they did share a common vision for peace in Panama. Though Torrijos was not entirely happy with the final treaties, he
said that he signed them "to save the lives of forty thousand Panamanians," implying the violence he had promised if no treaty were achieved.

The two new Panama Canal treaties abrogated the original 1903 treaty
as well as all subsequent agreements regarding the canal. The first treaty,
which was set to expire at noon on December 31, 1999, implemented a
number of important changes. A new organization, the Panama Canal
Commission, with five American and four Panamanian members, was
created to run the canal during the treaty period. The position of its com-
missioner would go to a Panamanian in 1990. Another bilateral body, the
Panama Canal Consultative Committee, was created to advise the respec-
tive governments on policy matters affecting the canal's operation.

Concretely, the treaty called for the number of skilled Panamanians
working on the canal to be steadily increased via U.S.-funded training
and for employees' right to join labor unions and to engage in collective
bargaining to be guaranteed. The amount of annual canal revenue that
Panama received was increased to $10 million and the amount per ship-
ton was increased as well. Lastly, the two countries agreed to a joint study
of a possible sea-level canal, which would address the canal's width
shortcomings.

The second treaty, a much shorter document, described the permanent
neutrality of the Panama Canal and both countries' right to defend it. The
treaty specifically guaranteed that both U.S. and Panamanian ships would
have "expeditious" transit in times of war. But since this treaty had no
expiration date and since Panama's Navy was infinitesimally smaller
(about a half dozen patrol craft) and weaker than the U.S. Navy, the language was a tacit recognition of U.S. inferred, if potential, sovereignty
over the canal.

Most urban Panamanians enthusiastically supported the treaties in a
national plebiscite that was inspired by the country's "millennial religion," the dream of sovereignty.[21] However, information about the treaties
was kept to a minimum. Some of the rural provinces, the city of Colón,

and the San Blas Islands in fact voted "no," apparently out of fear that a U.S. pull-out would destabilize the economy and remove a check against their own government's corruption and abuse. Many rural votes were mysteriously lost.

However, signing the treaty was only the first step. The true test was getting the approval of the treaties by the U.S. Senate. Carter faced an uphill battle against substantial resistance arrayed against the treaties among conservatives. Many hawks, with the Vietnam defeat still fresh in their minds, viewed the Panama Canal treaties as "another retreat." Carter rallied public support for the treaties, even bringing Torrijos himself to Washington to publicly demonstrate Panama's cooperative intentions.

The three-month-long debate in the Senate was boisterous and contentious, and was the longest in the history of the U.S. Senate. The discontent focused mainly on the Neutrality Treaty and pitted the conservatives against the combined forces of Carter's team and Panama's small, but effective, contingent. Carter used a very personal touch, including logic, cajoling, and political arm-twisting, to convince many individual senators to support the treaties. His staff gave close to one thousand information sessions to sway influential citizens toward support of the treaties in the hope that they would, in turn, sway their senators. Questions regarding Torrijos's and Noriega's illicit activities and human-rights abuses as well as their CIA connections were sidestepped or downplayed.

Carter worked up to the last minute during the final hours of Senate debate on the treaties, furiously manning the phones to shore up support from fence-sitters in Congress. Any time a senator would evoke a negative statement during the debates, Carter would literally run down the hallways to find support to counter the "setback."[22] Less than a day before the Senate was to vote, the entire process almost ground to a halt when Senator Dennis DeConcini of Arizona demanded an addition to the Neutrality Treaty in order to get his and four other senators' votes. This "condition" inserted a diplomatic understanding that stipulated that if the canal were ever threatened after Panama's assumption, the United States reserved the right to intervene militarily.

In Panama, Torrijos listened intently to the debates, which were broadcast live on National Public Radio. He was doubly enraged at DeConcini's proposal, because the two had met in Panama, and Torrijos felt betrayed. Each time DeConcini would address his condition, Torrijos would smash the radio in rage, and ended up going through a whole case of transmitters. For Torrijos, the swelling debate and need to portray himself as a benign dictator had unintended affects as he was forced to open up the country to political debate for the first time in a decade. Protests were on the rise against both the DeConcini condition and Torrijos's domestic policy. Reliably, students took to the streets, but they were not met by the National Guard. The mood in Panama was changing.

After much wrangling and political promises, the DeConcini condition was watered down, and the U.S. Senate finally ratified the treaties on April 18, 1978. Its passage occurred because 68 senators and the Joint Chiefs of Staff came to agree with Carter that Panama's consent, and not U.S. force, would be the best way to guarantee the canal's security. The Department of Defense had admitted that the canal could not be defended from internal threats of sabotage, which were most likely to emanate from Panama, not from an external aggressor.

Likewise easing the decision was the fact that the importance of the canal around the world was declining, and its economic and strategic importance to the United States had diminished considerably. Both the largest U.S. military ships, such as aircraft carriers, and an increasing fleet of oversized civilian cargo and oil supertankers were too large to use the Panama Canal. By 1976, some 7 percent of the world's commercial ships could not traverse the canal, and another 20 percent was restricted to one-way passage through the canal's narrow Culebra Cut.

Carter visited the Canal Zone to explain the treaties to Zonians whose livelihoods were to be changed. He had invested tremendous political capital in getting the treaties ratified, so much that it is considered to be a contributing factor to his losing the U.S. presidency in 1980. Likewise, Torrijos faced a loss of political support in Panama.

Surviving the Victory

The approval of the Panama Canal treaties was a doubled-edged sword for Torrijos. He had invested tremendous political capital into ensuring their passage, even using the issue as a rallying cry for Panama's population. In October 1978, a decade after the government declared political parties illegal in the aftermath of the 1968 military coup d'état, the 1972 Constitution was amended to create a new electoral law and to legalize political parties. To aid the liberalization, exiled political leaders, including Arnulfo Arias, were allowed to return. Political activity reached a new high, and a flurry of political activity was evident during the subsequent eighteen months. But with the canal now to become Panama's at the end of 1999, and with no outside power on which to blame Panama's problems, Torrijos was left without a rallying point for Panama's population.

To cool Panamanians' anger but yet maintain some control, Torrijos sought to transition toward a semi-open system similar to that existing in

Mexico. In Mexico, that country's Institutional Revolutionary Party (PRI) had been the dominant institution in an officially multiparty democratic system. But in practice, the PRI had dominated most aspects of society, and through institutionalization of its rule had been able to maintain the political gains made due to the revolutionary upheavals. Torrijos had in fact modeled many of his earlier social and economic reforms after similar reforms in Mexico. Most important and very ironic, Torrijos realized the need to reduce the National Guard's politics influence if he and his reforms were to last.

The result was the Democratic Revolutionary Party (PRD), which became Panama's semi-official party. Created in the house of Torrijos's friend, Rodrigo "Rory" González, the party was to serve as a transition vehicle to extricate the military from the government. The opening began in 1978 with a number of liberalizations. A civilian president, Arístides Royo, was appointed, though Torrijos still maintained control of policy matters. Law No. 81 was implemented, which legalized opposition political parties and liberated the media from major censorship and restrictions. The principal opposition newspaper, *La Prensa*, was founded by Roberto Eisenmann in August 1980. It provided the political opposition with its first venue of protest in over a decade.

The PRD was the first party to be officially recognized under the registration process that began in 1979. Though the political arena was ostensibly open, the only other political party able to surmount the still-in-effect Law of 30,000 during the first two years of Royo's term (1978–1980) was the Christian Democrats, who posed little threat to the PRD's overwhelming dominance. Other parties that made respectable showings were the Authentic Panamanianist Party (PPA), under the leadership of the venerable Arnulfo Arias, and the communist People's Party. Interestingly, another party, the People's Broad Front party (FAP) was created as the "official" opposition party, but it was in fact controlled by Torrijos himself.

However, a true opening did occur immediately. As the official party, the PRD wielded considerable sway over vast swathes of Panamanian society. It doled out government jobs and labor contracts and had access to public funds to recruit and hold its membership. This advantage was not shared with the opposition parties, which were doubly handicapped by the fact that Torrijos was only slowly opening up the system. In the first "open elections" in 1980, only 19 of the 57 seats in the National Legislation Council (Consejo Nacional de Legislación) were contested, while the rest remained in the hands of the Assembly and Torrijos, who appointed its representatives. In March 1979, a broad coalition of eight different leftist and rightist parties joined together in the National Opposition Front (FRENO) just to present a coherent front against the PRD for the 1980 legislative elections.

Though the democratic process had begun, the election had demonstrated that even liberalized, Panamanian politics was still too fragmented to pose a real threat to Torrijos's regime. Nonetheless, to the outside world, Panama's democratic façade was looking more respectable.

INTRANSIGENCE AND SHOOTING STARS

At the beginning of the 1980s, Torrijos's development programs began to lose steam under a stagnating economy. Though social spending had produced the highest educated and the healthiest population in Central America, it had come at a tremendous economic and social cost. Panama had taken out 12 successive loans from the International Monetary Fund and had accumulated over $1 billion in debt, reaching 12 percent of GDP. Accordingly, the country's income disparity was second in Central America only to El Salvador, and rural poverty had increased through the late 1970s by almost 50,000 families.

To secure further financial assistance, Torrijos was forced to moderate and accept business leaders' suggestions for policy changes, thus opening the regime up to more outside influences. He rolled back some of his statist policies, which resulted in increased unemployment rates. Political adhesion was lost, and despondency replaced fervor. Additionally, Torrijos had embroiled Panama in a number of unsavory regional situations. Panama was aiding the Sandinistas in Nicaragua as well as rebel forces throughout the region. Torrijos's rule became ever more tenuous as workers and students openly rebelled against the system.

Torrijos planned to fully democratize Panama's system in 1984 with open elections, partly to relieve the building social tension but mostly because of his concern about his National Guard officers. They were not enthusiastic about relinquishing power and were becoming less trustworthy and more suspect in their intentions. Torrijos had tried to give the officers a sense of mission and purpose, but the involvement in the Central American crisis had made Panama City a more nefarious place, where National Guard involvement in illegal arms and drugs sales was commonplace. To make matters worse, Torrijos's regime again became the target of U.S. criticism and pressure, this time from the newly elected U.S. president, Ronald Reagan, whose conservative administration sought to eradicate leftist movements throughout the Caribbean basin.

By the summer of 1981, Torrijos was openly dissatisfied with the progress his liberalization program was making, though he was reluctant to go any quicker for fear of a countercoup. But on July 31, 1981, Torrijos's 13 years of rule came to an unexpected end. Torrijos's small Canadian-made De Havilland Twin Otter plane crashed into a mountainside in western Panama. How it happened remains a mystery, though the assumption that someone assassinated him is popular. On the other hand, the premise that the crash was a pure accident is equally plausible—Torrijos was reckless and frequently eschewed caution and prudence. The weather the night of his fateful flight was stormy, and Torrijos would not have had any reservations about flying in bad weather; it would have reinforced his machismo.

What is certain is that Torrijos's death had a ripple effect through Panamanian society. Some celebrated his passing, but the thin veneer of legitimacy that Torrijos had created was stripped away. Panama's future was cast in doubt, and the incipient democratic movement was to become the prostrate servant of the dictatorship of Manuel Noriega.

NOTES

1. R. M. Koster and Guillermo Sánchez, *In the Time of the Tyrants* (New York: W. W. Norton Co., 1990), 74.

2. William J. Jorden, *Panama Odyssey* (Austin: University of Texas Press, 1984), 138.

3. U.S. Senate Committee on Foreign Relations, *Panama Canal Treaties: Hearings*, Exec N., 95th Congress, 1st session, 1977, part III, 97–101.

4. U.S. Department of Defense, secret memorandum to Zbigniew Brzezinsky, Special Assistant for National Security, October 14, 1977.

5. Robert A. Pastor, *Exiting the Whirlpool: U.S. Foreign Policy Toward Latin American and the Caribbean* (Boulder, CO: Westview Press, 2001), 2–4.

6. U.S. Ambassador Ambler Moss, Jr., interview by author, Miami, FL, April 17, 1997.

7. Omar Torrijos, *La Batalla de Panamá* (Buenos Aires: Editorial Universitaria de Buenos Aires, 1973): 12–16 and Frederick Kempe, *In the Time of Tyrants* (New York: G. Putnam's Sons, Inc., 1990), 68–70.

8. William L. Furlong and Margaret E. Scranton, *The Dynamics of Foreign Policymaking: The President, the Congress, and the Panama Canal Treaties* (Boulder, CO: Westview Press, 1984), 193–196.

9. Koster and Sánchez, 218.

10. Ricaurte Soler, *Panama: nación y oligarquía* (Panama City: Ediciones Tareas, 1987), 45–46.

11. Andrew Zimbalist and John Weeks, *Panama at the Crossroads: Economic Development and Political Change in the Twentieth Century* (Berkeley: University of California Press, 1991), 33.

12. Harry Johnson, "Panama as a Regional Financial Center: A Preliminary Analysis of Development Contribution." *Economic Development and Cultural Change*, XXIV (January 1976): 284.

13. Frederick Kempe, *Divorcing the Dictator* (New York: G. P. Putnam's Sons, 1990), 81.

14. John Dinges, *Our Man in Panama* (New York: Random House, 1990), 50.

15. *New York Times*, May 5, 1988.

16. *Newsweek*, June 18, 1973 and FBI Document # 180-10131-10342, November 3, 1978

17. Robert A. Pastor, *Exiting the Whirlpool: U.S. Foreign Policy Toward Latin American and the Caribbean* (Boulder, CO: Westview Press, 2001), 43.

18. Jorden, 452.

19. Graham Greene, *Getting to Know the General* (Thorndike, ME: Thorndike Press, 1984), 70–80.

20. Harold Molineu, *U.S. Policy Toward Latin America: From Regionalism to Globalism* (Boulder, CO: Westview Press, 1990), 144–145.

21. Koster and Sánchez, 189.

22. U.S. Ambassador Ambler Moss, Jr., interview by author, Miami, FL, April 17, 1997.

6

The Noriega Years, 1981–1990

The sudden death of Omar Torrijos was a shock to Panamanian society. No constitutional means to transfer power had been established, so a power vacuum appeared, as did great uncertainty about the future direction of the country. On the other hand, there were bright spots, as Panama had successfully obtained a treaty for the eventual control of the canal, which had done much to satisfy Panamanians' sense of nationalism. In addition, the United States had agreed to cease military interventions in Panamanian domestic affairs. But, as Graham Greene observed, Panamanians have traditionally been very pragmatic.[1] For their entire history as an independent state, both Panamanian officials and the population had balanced the economic benefits of the overwhelming U.S. presence with its impediment to true sovereignty for Panama. Torrijos's dramatic societal changes and the canal treaties had for the first time given the country a glimpse of that sovereignty. However, these gains were to be short lived without his commanding presence.

Torrijos had desired a transition away from dictatorship, because he believed that eventually it would be difficult to "get the gorillas back in the cage," as his used to muse to confidants about long-lasting dictatorships.[2] His philosophy had been backed by action. Shortly before his death he had instituted a series of democratic openings that slowly allowed for greater political participation and increasingly more open elections that were to culminate in an ostensibly open presidential election in 1984.

To ensure Panama's independence, Torrijos had both built nationalistic solidarity within Panama and fomented a strong alliance with other Latin American states that was meant to keep U.S. power within Panama at arm's length. Appropriately enough, John Dinges equates Panama City of the Torrijos era with Morocco during World War II: It was a no-holds-barred zone of foreign intrigue, clandestine activity, and money and arms dealing.[3] A tangible metaphor of this independence from U.S. dominance was the Colón Free Trade Zone, which had become a bountiful bazaar of illicit trade, especially with Cubans seeking to obtain much-sought-after U.S. computer technology forbidden by the U.S. embargo against the island.

Notwithstanding his shadowy aspects, Torrijos left behind a positive legacy, and the signing of the Panama Canal treaties had presaged better times. Between 1977 and 1981, Panama's GDP had grown by 5 percent annually and canal traffic by almost nine percent. Social indicators improved equally well. The average lifespan had increased to 71 years, and literacy campaigns and school building had contributed to a literacy rate of nearly 90 percent. Though revenues from canal traffic had increased substantially, to $60 million a year by the early 1980s, much of Torrijos's social and economic development—generous labor benefits, price controls, and a world-class banking center—as well as political support had been built upon foreign-financed loans, which was unsustainable in the long run. By the time of Torrijos's death, Panama possessed the highest per capita foreign debt in the Western Hemisphere.

As Walter LaFeber notes, the 1978 treaties changed little in the short term and, ironically, left Panama as dependent as ever on the United States, particularly in food exports.[4] Many major agricultural exports were either controlled by U.S. companies, such as United Brands, or their exports were largely directed to U.S. markets. By the mid-1970s, advancements in transport technology, such as supertankers, had gradually made the canal less important.

For the United States, the Panama Canal and the former Canal Zone no longer held their previous economic and strategic importance. The development of a two-ocean navy and nuclear missiles greatly reduced the canal's strategic importance and the necessity of maintaining military bases there. Furthermore, the development of improved ground transportation within the United States reduced the commercial importance of the canal. By the 1960s, Latin American countries, not the United States, were the primary users of the canal, and by the early 1980s, less than

1 percent of the U.S. gross national product was dependent on the Panama Canal.

But for Panama, the situation was mixed. While the gross receipts from canal tolls had increased from $57 million in 1963 to $303 million in 1981, the total number of transits was down 19 percent over the same time period, as a growing percentage of ships were too large to pass through the canal. In real terms, canal revenue had fallen almost 20 percent. The canal was increasingly subject to the whims of the U.S. market, the changing patterns of world trade, and, most importantly, the political winds in Washington.

Whereas the Panama Canal treaties had been expected to be the beginning of greater independence of Panama from Washington, the opposite was in fact true. The decade of the 1980s was characterized by even more interplay, conflict, and power brokering between the United States and the isthmus than any time since Panama's independence. Thus, the history of Panama during the 1980s, even more so than in previous decades, is really the story of relations between the two countries.

Domestically, Panama's relative political inexperience left it open to abuse at the hands of leaders less visionary and less restrained than Torrijos. Panamanian society had been radically changed during his rule, but its transformation was incomplete and therefore vulnerable to exploitation. Soon after Torrijos's death his junior officers began to struggle for leadership of the country. Though many of them had their sights on replacing Torrijos, it was Manuel Noriega, the Torrijos-appointed head of the Panamanian G-2 intelligence unit, who eventually assumed command of both the military and the country. Noriega's corrupt, Machiavellian dictatorship would usher the country into its worst period of violence and economic ruin in its modern history.

NORIEGA TAKES CHARGE

Noriega was born poor and illegitimate in 1936 in a Panama City slum. Derisively nicknamed *cara de piña* (pineapple face) because of his pronounced acne pockmarks, Noriega did not get many breaks until his half-brother, Luis Carlos, a minor official at Panama's embassy in Lima, got him a scholarship in 1958 to Peru's Chorrillo military academy. Noriega received training in psychological operations at Fort Bragg in 1967 and attended a two-month course in military intelligence at the School of the Americas in Panama. While still in Peru, Noriega began a long relationship as a paid informant to the U.S. Central Intelligence Agency (CIA), relaying tips on possible communists at the academy. This began a relationship with the CIA that would continue almost unabated for 30 years. Though temporarily dropped from the CIA payroll during Jimmy Carter's administration, Noriega was reinstated at the beginning of the 1980s by the Reagan administration, and even received a raise to $200,000 annually.

After graduation, Noriega was given an officer appointment in the National Guard under Omar Torrijos and became Panama's chief of intelligence, expanding his intelligence and black market contacts with both friends and foes of the United States: Cubans, Israelis, Taiwanese, and Libyans, among others. Some officials at the U.S. State Department were aware of Noriega's ability to play Cuba and the United States off each other while remaining the supposed "neutral" intermediary. For this reason, to many in the U.S. government, Noriega came to be known as the "rent-a-colonel."

During the two years following Torrijos's death (1981–1983), four National Guard colonels, including Noriega, jostled for power. First was Florencio Flores, who held power for just eight months before being overthrown by his fellow officers. Next was Rubén Paredes, who became commander of the National Guard in March 1982. A Torrijos-era official, Paredes left Noriega, now a brigadier general, in control of the G-2 while other officers agreed to a plan that called for alternating power among the Guard's officers. Torrijos's plan for a democratic opening quietly faded away.

Increasing labor strikes and growing public discontent against the Torrijos-appointed administration of Arístides Royo led to his ouster by Paredes and the National Guard on July 30, 1982. Royo's replacement, Vice President Ricardo de la Espriella, no doubt recognizing that his presidency was dependent on appeasing the National Guard, formed a government filled with military-friendly PRD members. He openly referred to the military as his "partner in power." But while the civilians acted as administrators, almost every important sector of Panama's economy and government remained firmly in the hands of the National Guard. The PRD, the "official" political party begun under Torrijos, had in fact become a political front for the National Guard. However, as a simple vehicle of the military's whims, the PRD was not openly accepted by those outside its corporate reach and carried little legitimacy outside its own membership.

In April 1983 a national referendum was held on amendments to Torrijos's 1972 constitution approved the previous year. Among the more important changes was the prohibition against National Guard members participating in elections and the provision for direct election of legislators.

In accordance with one of these new rules, Paredes resigned his command to run for president in August 1983, which put Noriega in command of the National Guard. Paredes had been one of Torrijos's top choices to take over after the general's retirement, and Paredes envisioned himself something of a new Torrijos, publicly stating that he was the country's new "strong man" and that he was going be a "unifier." He criticized Royo for Panama's dire economic downturn and made allegations that government officials had embezzled funds from the national social security system. Paredes, however, never gained widespread support from PRD loyalists and had only minimal support from the Partido Liberal, which had allied itself with the PRD.

A popular Panamanian saying explains Paredes's predicament: "Power is a viper; you must release it slowly or it will bite you." Paredes was bitten as Noriega seized upon the power vacuum and promoted himself to the rank of general. His first major act was to enact new legislation, called Law 20, which renamed the National Guard the Panamanian Defense Forces (PDF) and tripled its size to 15,000 soldiers. Law 20 also gave the PDF a mission to protect the canal against communist insurgency, which was meant to curry favor from the United States in the form of even more financial support for his fledgling military. The PDF received a wide assortment of U.S. military equipment, including light infantry tanks and machine guns.

But aside from material gains, Law 20 also provided the new PDF with the legal means to control many important sectors of civilian life: Immigration, transportation, railroads, and airports were all brought under military supervision. Recognizing that he no longer had the military's support, less than a month after he began Paredes withdrew as the PRD candidate (though he would appear on the ballot as a minor candidate for the Popular Nationalist Party—PNP). Noriega, now the de facto leader, named the former World Bank vice president, Nicolás Ardito Barletta, as the official PRD presidential candidate. Noriega and the other officers had grown too used to power and privilege to give them away.

Reaction in the United States as well as in Panama to Noriega's power grab was mixed. There was still no broad-reaching political party structure in Panama that could counter the PDF, and the U.S. Cold War policy of tolerating, if not supporting, stable though brutal Latin American dictatorships made Noriega acceptable. In addition, Noriega was known to many in Washington's policymaking community since he had attended seven different military training sessions at the School of the Americas in the Panama Canal Zone. However, the most likely reason that the United States assumed Noriega's trustworthiness was that since 1967 he had been receiving a $110,000 annual salary as a CIA informant, which had been ordered by the new U.S. vice president, George H. W. Bush, when he was head of the CIA. President Reagan's personal crusade against communism in Central America helped Noriega find favor, since the Reagan administration viewed Central America as the U.S. "backyard" and the most likely place for communist infiltration, an assumption seemingly substantiated by Nicaragua's 1979 Sandinista Revolution.

Both Noriega and Torrijos had CIA connections, but the similarity ended there. While U.S. officials had viewed Torrijos as contradictory to U.S. interests, Noriega was perceived by Washington officials as loyal and pliant. Noriega worked closely with a variety of U.S. agencies: the Drug Enforcement Administration, the Department of Defense, the CIA, and even the White House, supplying intelligence and allowing Panamanian territory to be used by Americans and the anti-Sandinista Contras for the U.S. war against communism in Central America. Noriega also conveniently ignored the fact that the presence of SOUTHCOM, the U.S. military command for Latin America located in the former Canal Zone, violated the canal treaties. His cooperative demeanor brought increased financial assistance to Panama from the United States as well as personal wealth to Noriega himself. During the last years of Torrijos's rule, financial assistance from the United States had practically evaporated. But after Noriega assumed control, U.S. aid rose over 600 percent, to $15 million annually.

Noriega also had a substantially different personality than his former boss. He was not inspired by social or nationalist ideals. Instead of Torrijos's stern father-figure persona, Noriega was more of a street thug who thrived on dread, vice, corruption, and fleeting material and carnal passions. From his first position of power as a head of the city of David's traffic police, Noriega was perverse in his use of power to humiliate prisoners and blackmail citizens. Once in the higher echelons of power, Noriega did not seek a greater good for Panama but power and money for himself, and Panama became his personal vehicle for wealth. Noriega, like Torrijos, showered the Panamanian people with propaganda that the military regime was protected under a "Pentagon umbrella" and was the best protection of Panama's sovereignty.[5] However, the true nature of the regime was more apparent to those outside its grasp. An Israeli intelligence agent who knew Noriega well described the country during the dictator's rule: "Panama is a funny country . . . it's not really a country. It's more like a business . . . I know the storekeeper."[6]

In addition to his intelligence connections, Noriega's early rule was greatly facilitated by geopolitical circumstances and changing U.S. policy toward Latin America. The Reagan administration radically changed U.S.

policy toward Latin America away from the multilateral approaches favored by Carter toward more bilateral support for anti-communist regimes in Latin America, regardless of their democratic or humanitarian characteristics. Particularly after Nicaragua's 1979 revolution, Panama and its military became a centerpiece of U.S. policy as a seemingly faithful ally in the struggle against communism in Central America. This made Noriega a key component in U.S. policy in the region.

To bolster his anti-communist credentials, Noriega allowed the United States to set up listening posts in Panama and to train the anti-Sandinista Contras in western Panama near the border with Costa Rica. He also acted as an intermediary with Cuba's Fidel Castro. Though some Reagan administration policies were increasingly detrimental to Panamanian sovereignty, such as reassuming control of Panama Canal funds (which in 1977 had been given to a joint U.S.-Panama commission), Noriega was unfazed and utilized U.S. fears of communist incursion in Central America to his own benefit. With U.S. aid and trust in his back pocket, Noriega audaciously reorganized Panamanian politics to his liking. The PDF openly controlled the country, and Noriega was established as the power behind the throne.

Facing this radicalization was a more educated and more middle-class Panamanian society that demanded more, not less, liberalization. But Panamanians' call for change was frequently met brutally by Noriega's new anti-riot police, nicknamed "Dobermans," whose training had been funded by the U.S. military aid. All hope of a democratic transition, no matter how much the United States proclaimed to promote it, died with Torrijos.

THE FAÇADE CRUMBLES

That fact that Noriega's rise to power had been facilitated and welcomed by many sectors of the U.S. government did not stop him from coming under scrutiny. In January 1980 the U.S. Federal Bureau of Investigation (FBI) opened an investigation into Noriega's illicit dealings and found that at the direction of Noriega and Torrijos, Panamanian buyers had purchased $10 million in weapons destined for the Nicaragua's new Sandinista government. This was not, however, news to the U.S. government, which had known that Noriega had been involved in drug trafficking since at least 1972, when the Nixon administration had considered assassinating him. Nonetheless, Noriega had remained on the payrolls of the CIA and U.S. military intelligence services. On one occasion in 1979, Noriega was shielded by the U.S. military from drug-trafficking prosecution in Florida and given a payment of $12 million to provide safe haven on Panama's Contadora Island to the deposed Shah of Iran.

This convoluted U.S. relationship with Noriega continued into 1983 when a U.S. Senate committee concluded that Panama was a major center for the laundering of drug funds and drug trafficking. But the same year, by facilitating weapons shipments to Managua, Noriega helped Robert McFarlane and John Poindexter of the U.S. National Security Council sidestep the Boland Amendment, a U.S. law that prohibited any type of military assistance to the Contras to overthrow Nicaragua's Sandinista government. Under Noriega's direction, the money for what became known as the "Iran-Contra Affair" was laundered through Panama's banks and shell companies, and the anti-Sandinista Contras received training at a base in western Panama. Noriega also facilitated the CIA airlift of weapons to the Contras. Arranged by the United States, weapons from Israel went to secret airstrips that Noriega had established in both Honduras and Costa Rica during the 1970s when the National Guard was smuggling weapons to the Sandinistas. These same airstrips were later used by Noriega to facilitate a drug-trafficking arrangement with Colombia's notorious Medallín Cartel, a business he had begun in the early 1980s.

Through the mid-1980s, the Reagan administration collected reams of intelligence that proved Noriega's drug-trafficking connections conclusively, but his help in fighting Nicaragua's Sandinista regime protected him from prosecution. Noriega was, in fact, playing on both sides of the fence for his own financial benefit. While purportedly helping the United States fight regional communism, Noriega expanded his business and intelligence contacts with both the Sandinistas and the Cubans. He correctly understood that, at the time, the United States cared more about fighting the Sandinistas than about waging a war against drugs.

THE 1984 ELECTION

The 1984 presidential elections in Panama were meant to give Noriega's regime a modicum of legitimacy, even though constitutional changes made the previous year ensured that real power would remain in the hands of the PDF. Instead, the election demonstrated Noriega's ability to undermine the political process and to strip away the remaining shreds of democracy.

Noriega's hand-picked PRD candidate, Nicolás Ardito Barletta, headed a six-party coalition ticket called the National Democratic Union (UNADE). Opposing Ardito Barletta was 83-year-old Arnulfo Arias, who had reemerged for a fourth presidential bid. Fronting his own left-leaning co-alition, called the Democratic Opposition Alliance (ADO), Arias had toned down his anti-U.S. rhetoric and was now directing his attacks at the PDF, calling for their withdrawal from all public sectors of Panamanian life.

Even so, Ardito Barletta was clearly favored by the United States. He had earned a Ph.D. in economics from the University of Chicago, where Reagan's secretary of state, George Schultz, had been his professor. The selection of a trained economist as the presidential candidate was not coincidental. In 1984 Panama experienced its first year of negative economic growth in 33 years and unemployment was over 10 percent. In addition, foreign debt payments were still devouring a sizable portion of the budget, consuming almost 9 percent of the GDP. To complicate matters, the United States had reduced imports from the Caribbean, including Panama, by 84 percent since 1981.[7]

Both sides predicted certain victory, but Arias, no matter how much his discourse might have changed, was not going to be given a fair chance. The PDF began a campaign of blatant coercion of government officials and opposition leaders into accepting Ardito Barletta as the official candidate. It was also the start of the erosion of the foundation of the carefully built multiclass coalition that composed the PRD alliance, as its members increasingly quarreled over political space and the country's future. Buried beneath the fury of the election campaign was the forced resignation of President Ricardo de la Espriella, who had been vocal in his opposition to the PDF's interference in the election. He was briefly succeeded by Vice President Jorge Illueca.

The confusion and dissension that resulted was encouraged by Noriega, since it helped his plans to tighten his grip on control of the country as rival groups lashed out at each other. The PDF controlled almost all of the media and used it to blanket the country with pro-UNADE messages. Only the fiercely independent La Prensa and its vociferous editor, Roberto Eisenmann, supported Arias's ADO coalition. The United States also helped tilt the playing field in Ardito Barletta's favor by contributing funds to his campaign via the National Endowment for Democracy, an organization funded by the U.S. Congress. Nonetheless, Ardito Barletta's campaigning tactics were questionable in that he utilized public funds for his campaign and made intimations of substantial layoffs of Panama's public workers if Arias were elected.

The election took place on May 6, 1984. The count dragged on for an inordinately long time, and rumors began to surface that the vote had been rigged. Arias's ADO brought charges before Panama's election tribunal that many votes for their candidate had been destroyed. These charges were summarily dismissed by Panama's Noriega-controlled electoral committee. But even under these irregular circumstances, the vote was very close. When it became possible that Arias could win, the vote tabulation was halted by Noriega while his PDF henchmen assisted with the recount. Violence and rioting broke out right in front of the Legislative Palace, leaving one person dead and forty others injured.

Over 2,000 plausible charges of vote manipulation and widespread vote buying in the countryside led to deep suspicion of the entire process. Both of Panama's electoral commissions demanded an investigation. But the bribing of two Panamanian Supreme Court justices by Noriega sealed Arias's fate, and Ardito Barletta was declared the winner by a scant 1,713 votes. When Arias's supporters took to the streets to protest the election, they were met by the PDF with deadly force.

The United States declared the election a "significant step forward toward democracy" and signaled its approval by sending Secretary of State Schultz to attend the new Panamanian president's inauguration. In accordance with the new "Reagan Doctrine," which started to promote democratic civilian leaders over military ones, the United States was more interested that a civilian continue the process of democratization begun by Torrijos, regardless of how that person took office. As such, Noriega had no reason to believe that his deception would be seriously challenged by the United States so long as he was cooperative in the anti-communism struggle. There was every indication that the U.S. policy of "stability-first, democracy-second" still applied to Panama, and Noriega was still considered by Washington policymakers as "their man in Panama."

THE SPADAFORA INCIDENT

Undoubtedly believing in his invulnerability, Noriega began to crack down on dissenters of all stripes. The saddest but most pivotal example of Noriega's brutality was the murder of Hugo Spadafora, a Panamanian physician and former official in the Torrijos government. Spadafora had raised volunteers in Panama and led them in the late 1970s against Nicaragua's Somoza regime, and had become something of a hero to many Panamanians in the process. But after the Sandinista victory, Spadafora became disillusioned with that regime's hard-line direction and, instead, began to help the anti-Sandinista Contras operating from Costa Rica. When Spadafora learned of Noriega's drug trafficking, he publicly denounced Noriega and planned to return to Panama to lead a protest against him. On September 13, 1985, Spadafora crossed from Costa Rica into Panama at his home province of Chiriquí. He was immediately pulled from his bus and arrested by Francisco Eliécer González Bonilla, a G-2 intelligence agent.

Spadafora's fate was spelled out in a phone call intercepted by the U.S. National Security Agency between Noriega, who was opportunely away in France, and Luis "Papo" Córdoba, the Chiriquí provincial commander. Córdoba declared, "We have the rabid dog," to which Noriega rhetorically responded, "And what does one do with a dog that has rabies?" Spadafora's decapitated and brutally tortured body was found the following day in Costa Rica just across the border from Panama. But more than an act of senseless brutality, Spadafora's murder proved to be the catalyst for Panama's opposition to confront Noriega's regime and began to drive a wedge between the regime and the United States.

Though he had been put in office under dubious circumstances, Ardito Barletta took his presidential role seriously. A studious technocrat, Ardito Barletta had set out to make his presidency an honest administration. In the face of Panama's enormous foreign debt, he announced austerity programs, promoted by the IMF and World Bank, that were deleterious to the country's economy. Students, workers, and even professional organizations took to the streets in huge protests, forcing the new president to back down from the measures less than two weeks later. Ardito Barletta held no legitimacy among most Panamanians, who called him *el fraudito* (the little fraud).

There was another reason Ardito Barletta had difficulty implementing policy. Though the military had ruled Panama for a decade and a half, Panamanian cultural norms had not changed noticeably. Ardito Barletta's efficient, no-nonsense style of governance conflicted with upper-class Panamanians' expectations of *manus manum lavat* as well as the military's traditional populist use of funds to appease the lower classes. The dictatorship was ripping Panama's social fabric at the seams.

While in New York renegotiating Panama's foreign debt, Ardito Barletta was questioned by U.S. reporters about Spadafora's murder. He promised to look into the matter, and upon his return he announced his intention to set up a commission to investigate it. This campaign for transparency fit nicely into Ardito Barletta steady lobbying of Noriega for greater personal freedoms, such as the rights to speech and assembly, for the Panamanian public. However, Ardito Barletta was ultimately caught between two irreconcilable forces: the military to whom he owed his presidency and the political opposition that saw him as feckless.[8]

In the end, no investigation occurred. Ardito Barletta was forced to resign as president after a combination of threats toward his family by Noriega's chief of staff, Roberto Díaz Herrera, and, purportedly, after being held a virtual prisoner in his presidential office by Noriega himself.[9] Noriega replaced Ardito Barletta with Vice President Eric Arturo Delvalle, who became the first in a line of puppet presidents, derisively called "Kleenex presidents" by Panamanians for their disposability. Noriega's regime was done trying to fake democracy, and a new struggle for power began in Panama, with its implications becoming obvious to U.S. officials. Delvalle's inauguration was boycotted by the U.S. ambassador to Panama, Everett Briggs, signaling the end of "business as usual."

Ardito Barletta had been offered as a sacrificial lamb to assuage both public and foreign ire. Austerity measures had reduced government spending by $128 million, which had resulted in extensive teacher and public worker layoffs. By 1985, debt service had reached 37 percent of government spending, rising from 29 percent in 1982. But the reductions had also required the sell-off of many public enterprises, putting many government workers, who made up a significant proportion of the workforce, out of work. Organized labor and public sector workers had historically formed the basis of political support for the Noriega regime, as it had under Torrijos.

Nonetheless, the resignation of Ardito Barletta was particularly problematic for Noriega, because Washington had high hopes for the financially savvy president who had been arranging for Panama to stay solvent in its $4 billion debt to U.S. lenders. To signal its displeasure, the United States reduced Panama's economic aid from $40 million to just $6 million. Ardito Barletta's dismissal began an increasingly serious spiral of domestic upheavals and U.S. scrutiny even as most U.S. anti-communism efforts in Central America continued to be based in Panama.

Though corrupt and vile, Noriega still had residual value for U.S. policy in the region. At the request of the CIA, Noriega was assisting Nicaraguan Contras with arms shipments that were funneled through Panama and by coordinating attacks on the Sandinistas. For his assistance, Noriega received $300,000 and an implicit understanding that Washington would turn a blind eye to his corruption.

PANAMA IN CRISIS

Over the next four years, Panama would endure a series of "mini-crises."[10] Spadafora's murder was perhaps the most important crisis, in that it was a catalyst that ignited public anger against the regime. This outcry was echoed by Panama's independent and rebellious newspaper, La Prensa, as well as by Spadafora's own influential family. But Noriega's stranglehold on Panamanian society made any real investigation doomed to failure. The editor of *La Prensa*, Roberto Eisenmann, fled Panama in 1986 under death threats. Such a blatant politically motivated murder, as well as the sacking of an elected president, made some in the U.S. State Department rethink the official U.S. "hands-off" approach to Noriega. To signal its displeasure, $14 million in U.S. aid originally bound for Panama was redirected to Guatemala, which had just elected a civilian president.[11]

Noriega's change in status from an ally of the United States to a public enemy was swift, though very little of the change was attributable to drug trafficking or a lack of democracy, since U.S. policy had explicitly removed drug trafficking from all intelligence reports on the country.[12] Noriega's sense of immunity from U.S. reprisal had given him the perceived freedom to act autonomously. But the autonomy began to be seen by some U.S. policymakers as potentially dangerous to the Panama Canal, which, although already scheduled to be turned over to Panama at the end of 1999, was still viewed by many in Washington as a strategically vital possession of the United States. While the United States wavered in its opinion of Noriega, Panama's streets began to erupt with the population's dissatisfaction with the man who was now the country's open dictator.

UNBINDING TIES

In 1986 fissures began to take form in Panama's political and economic system as well as in the U.S.-Panama relationship. The Noriega regime's cohesiveness splintered as supporters—both domestic and foreign—began to take sides in partisan conflicts. In December 1985, Noriega had been asked by the U.S. National Security Council's director, John Poindexter, to help scuttle the Contadora peace plan for Nicaragua, to reinstall Ardito Barletta (who had gone into exile in the United States), and provide safe haven to deposed Philippine dictator Ferdinand Marcos. Noriega's refusal to all these requests set in motion the machinery that would lead to his eventual downfall.

Angered by Noriega's rejection, Poindexter returned to the United States and got articles published in prominent U.S. newspapers about Noriega's drug-trafficking and money-laundering connections with Colombia's Medallín drug cartel. In addition, it had become quite clear that Noriega was playing both sides in the struggle against communism, since Cuban communiqués intercepted by U.S. intelligence referred to Noriega as *nuestro hombre* ("our man"). In particular, a series of *New York Times* articles meticulously outlined the general's nefarious activities. Noriega tried to rectify the mistake and made a counteroffer to infiltrate Nicaragua to assassinate the Sandinista leadership. But the damage to his credibility, as it were, had been done, and some U.S. officials began to abandon him.

The final straw was pulled when in the summer of 1986 the U.S. Congress reauthorized aid to Nicaragua's Contras, which made Noriega's cooperation in the anti-Sandinista struggle nonessential.[13] Concurrently, in the United States the 1986 Iran-Contra scandal had broken, and during testimony before the U.S. Congress Noriega's drug connections and his relationship with the United States were highlighted. Noriega became an embarrassment for the Reagan administration and was quickly transformed from "our man in Panama" to a symbol of anti-U.S. illicit activities in the region. The scandal removed what remaining protection from forces in the United States Noriega might have had left.

Inside Panama, citizens from practically all walks of life began to resist the dictatorship and protested against the United States for the lack of progress and cooperation by the U.S.-controlled Panama Canal Commission, which was slow to replace American administrators with Panamanians and increase canal payments. Though 82 percent of the canal workers were Panamanian, the white-collar jobs were still overwhelmingly held by Americans. Adding fuel to the fire, the arch-conservative U.S. senator Jesse Helms suggested that the United States should not honor the canal treaties, implying that Panama may be too unstable to run and safeguard the waterway. The fact that Panama's PRD ruling party had joined the Socialist International in June 1987 no doubt contributed to this consternation.

In response, the Reagan administration instituted a number of Panama-related initiatives that grated on Panamanians' sensibilities as much as the intractable Noriega regime had. The U.S. ambassador to Panama, Arthur Davis, publicly stated that "the success" of the turnover of the canal to Panama would be linked to the establishment of a democratic government, thus implying that the United States was prepared to not honor the canal treaties if Noriega were still in power. However, the statement is more correctly interpreted to convey the trepidation that many officials in the United States had about giving up strategically important U.S. military bases in Panama, which were to be closed and turned over to Panama as part of the treaty agreements.

The United States contributed to the growing crisis in a number of other ways. The U.S. government denied Panama's request for $54 million in canal profits, which purportedly was to proportionally equalize Panama's profit-cost ratio with that of the United States.[14] A series of probes were made by the United States to Panama's President Delvalle about possibly retaining the canal past the year 2000, which would have effectively nullified the treaties. In the most direct challenge to the canal treaty, Nicaraguan Contras were trained for anti-Sandinista conflict at Fort Sherman in the Canal Zone. The United States began openly challenging Panamanian sovereignty via unauthorized training exercises near the Panamanian cities of Herrera and Veraguas. Lastly, at the behest of the Reagan administration, the U.S. Congress approved legislation that gave the U.S. president the sole power to interpret the 1977 canal treaties for Panama. The perception of such a U.S. challenge to Panamanian sovereignty brought out huge joint demonstrations in the streets of Panamanian cities, ironically with citizens and soldiers walking together in a statement that Panama expected the canal turnover be fulfilled as stipulated in the treaties.

THE CRISIS BEGINS

The unity between the PDF and citizens was very short lived. The opposition press and media began a blitz against the Noriega regime and public demonstrations, and the reactionary violent repression by the PDF became more frequent. Interestingly, Noriega's own intransigence made enemies within his own military. Colonel Roberto Díaz Herrera (a cousin of Omar Torrijos) had been designated to succeed Noriega as the PDF commander, but Noriega reneged on the agreement and announced his intention to remain in charge for another five years.

An incensed Díaz Herrera sought revenge. He publicly accused Noriega of rigging the 1984 presidential elections, planning Torrijos's death, and ordering the murder of Hugo Spadafora. The last declaration sparked the largest public protest in Panamanian history. Díaz Herrera's defection created a severe rift inside the military regime, setting Torrijos-era loyalists against Noriega's followers. Noriega accused Díaz Herrera of participating in an antigovernment conspiracy and accused Diaz of "high treason." In the pre-dawn hours of July 27 soldiers of the PDF's *Batallión 2000* surrounded Díaz Herrera's house. After a brief but intense firefight, he was arrested and finally sent into exile in Venezuela.

Sparked by Díaz Herrera's accusations, which had been published in *La Prensa*, the National Civic Crusade (NCC) was born. Composed of 65 different organizations, including the Catholic Church, the NCC's strategy was civil disobedience, which was manifested by groups of citizens waving white handkerchiefs, cars incessantly blowing their horns, and housewives standing on patios and balconies banging kitchen pots in cacophonous protest.[15] Noriega asserted that the NCC was the brainchild of the U.S. embassy in Panama, which had supported the training of NCC leaders, and of Panama's *rabiblanco* elite, who Noriega said was anxious to see him replaced with a more pliant, conservative leader. The NCC was equally vociferous in its opposition to attempts by the International Monetary Fund and the World Bank to address the country's foreign debt burden by imposing draconian cuts on Panama's social security system, forcing the privatization of state companies, and reducing the public sector workforce.

The NCC also promoted large-scale labor strikes, which literally shut down Panama for weeks at a time. Noriega's intelligence network, however, was able to hobble some protests before they occurred, and Noriega's response to the strikes was direct and vicious. A state of emergency was declared, which suspended the writs of habeas corpus and allowed the PDF to destroy protesters' property and ransack the offices of *La Prensa*. All independent media were shut down or chose to stop operations in protest of the regime's censorship. All foreign correspondents were expelled from the country.

But the regime's violence, paradoxically, only fueled the growth in civic opposition groups. Even Panama's Catholic Church, traditionally apolitical, became openly critical of Noriega, particularly the Church's vocal archbishop, Marcos McGrath, who called for an impartial investigation of the allegations. Noriega responded with even more violence. For five days (June 9–14), riot police and antigovernment protesters clashed in the streets of Panama City. The PDF beat and jailed opposition leaders, fired birdshot into crowds, and released tear gas in restricted spaces. The remaining antigovernment television and radio stations, which had reported the disturbances, were shut down. Noriega's puppet president, Delvalle, issued a statement declaring a 10-day "state of siege," which officially suspended constitutional rights, giving the PDF the legal cover to continue with the crackdown. There were at least 1,000 arrested, more than 100 injured, and several reported deaths.

Noriega used the chaos to try to eliminate some of his potential opposition. The Noriega-controlled National Assembly issued a decree that some members of the Assembly, by supporting the protests, had committed "high treason" against the government. Nine prominent business leaders and opposition political leaders, including former President Ardito Barletta, were accused of being traitors and conspiring with the United States to overthrow Delvalle. On June 19 the state of emergency was extended indefinitely, which effectively created a state of marshal law in the country and removed all constitutional guarantees.

On July 7 President Delvalle announced a decree prohibiting demonstrations in public places, but the next day opposition protesters were again in the streets in defiance. On July 10 over 100,000 people, all dressed in white, filled the major thoroughfares of Panama City in peaceful protest. Noriega's anti-protest "Doberman" guards unleashed a torrent of buckshot on the crowd and prowled the city looking for sympathizers, sometimes pulling suspected protesters from their homes and beating them senseless on the sidewalk. The rampage became known in Panama as "Viernes Negro" (Black Friday).

The frenzied political environment caused at least one billion dollars in foreign investment to flee the country during the June to July uprisings, leaving the Panamanian treasury short and not able to meet financial obligations such as foreign debt, which had grown to a staggering $6 billion. During 1987, Panama had paid $800 million in debt service payments, which was equivalent to almost half its national budget. Unemployment had risen past 10 percent and continued to grow.

The crisis complicated the payback of Panama's foreign debt. The World Bank had proposed an austerity program in order to qualify for a $50 million bailout loan, and in 1985 Panama had agreed to reform its social security system, which was close to bankruptcy. Between 1985 and 1987, Panama had met other World Bank and International Monetary Fund program requirements and received loans totaling almost $200 million. But resistance to further reform in social security was widespread, as it would have left the average Panamanian with a smaller pension. In addition, inflation was increasing and housing shortages were appearing. A poll taken by the Gallup Organization in the summer of 1987 showed that three-quarters of Panamanians wanted Noriega to leave power.

The public response from the U.S. government to the growing chaos in Panama was highly critical. At the end of July 1987 the U.S. Senate passed a nonbinding resolution that called for Noriega to step down and ordered all military aid to the PDF terminated. Arthur Davis, the U.S. ambassador to Panama, was sent to the home of the an opposition leader, Ricardo Arias Calderón, which plainly signaled a U.S. retraction of support from Noriega. More nationalist Panamanian leaders responded to this meeting with charges that the United States was interfering in Panama's domestic affairs.

Panama's National Assembly demanded the expulsion of the U.S. ambassador and accused the United States of interventionist aggression. Noriega capitalized on the anger by sending about 500 Panamanian public workers to protest in front of the U.S. embassy in Panama City, which they pelted with stones and splattered with red paint, resulting in considerable property destruction. However, many of the workers had simply participated out of fear of losing their jobs, which were contingent on demonstrating loyalty to Noriega.

The U.S. secretary of state, Elliot Abrams, publicly asked the PDF to remove Noriega, implying that the reinstatement of U.S. financial assistance might be the reward. However, the fairly cohesive PDF officer corps was not enticed, and with good reason: Since the early 1970s it had benefited financially from the two dictatorships (Torrijos and Noriega) and had been tapping profits from a variety of government agencies. Also, as Steve Ropp notes, its growth in size from a small paramilitary force of 5,500 in the late 1960s to a well-armed and more professional military of 16,000 in the mid-1980s gave it more autonomy from U.S. pressure.[16]

The Delvalle government expressed its indignation at the intervention by calling a special session of the Organization of American States (OAS) on July 1 to protest U.S. interventionism in Central America, including Panama. Seventeen Latin American states voted in favor of condemnation of the action, while only the United States voted against the measure. Behind the scenes, the United States gave Noriega a variety of options to step down quietly, but as it turned out, too many options. Noriega played one negotiator against the other, obviously never intending to leave power.

The United States then channeled $90,000 to the National Civic Crusade, again through the National Endowment for Democracy. These funds educated and helped opponents of Noriega to develop strategies for resisting the regime,[17] but this training led to more direct confrontations. At least three university students were shot by riot police, and on October 3, 1987, over two thousand teachers demonstrated in Panama City, demanding improvements in the country's school system. A larger strike scheduled for two weeks later was broken up by over one thousand soldiers, but the same day the public's frustration at the regime boiled over in an indirect act against the regime: An electrical transmission tower providing most of Panama City's electricity was bombed, plunging the city into darkness.

Though the Delvalle government had banned public protests, it was through many arrests and rampant coercion that Noriega was able to hobble civic organizations' leaders sufficiently, and the number of protests dwindled. Among those arrested were 11 U.S. soldiers for purportedly vandalizing Panamanian property. Noriega's targets were expanded to include Delvalle's own vice president, Roderick Esquivel, whose offices were ransacked after his Liberal Party withdrew from its coalition with ruling PRD. For the next two years, Panama's courts held virtually no criminal trials. Detainees, many of whom were political opponents of Noriega's dictatorship, were jailed without charges.

Sensing the severity of the crisis, the U.S. Congress voted unanimously to cut off all economic and military aid to Panama, and all U.S.-related multilateral agencies were instructed to vote against aid of any type to Panama in international economic fora.[18] The World Bank, in which the United States has a strong voice, canceled a $50 million loan to Panama. This type of economic warfare was especially tailored to affect Panama, since upto 90 percent of its foreign monetary transactions are conducted through the United States and over half of all private sector business is related to the United States. Since between 30 percent and 40 percent of Panama's national budget was dedicated to paying its foreign debt, this type of sanction would, in theory, cripple Panama's ability to get new credit.

In December 1987 the Reagan administration sent Deputy Secretary of State Richard Armitage to give Noriega the message that all branches of the U.S. government were now united in demanding his resignation. After Noriega's refusal, the United States countered by eliminating sugar quotas from Panama, which resulted in the closing of one-third of Panama's sugar mills and threatened the family fortune of President Delvalle, whose family wealth was based on the sugar industry. In addition, exposés of Noriega began appearing in the U.S. media, particularly the *New York Times* and the *Los Angeles Times*.

In retaliation, the Panamanian government ordered all U.S. employees of the U.S. International Development (USAID) out of the country. The U.S. actions, which were meant to pressure Noriega to leave, were actually counterproductive in that they actually helped Noriega by allowing him to claim that he was protecting Panamanian national sovereignty from the "imperial actions" of the United States.[19] At the end of 1987, Panama was in a state of persistent social upheaval and its economy was in shambles. Panama had lost over $80 million in U.S. aid in 1987 alone. Perhaps to bolster his bargaining position with the United States, Noriega allowed the Soviet Union to use Panamanian dry-dock facilities and was negotiating with Libya for financial assistance.

THE CRISIS DEEPENS

The turning point in the building crisis was the February 1988 pronouncement in the United States that declared drug trafficking a major threat to American society. Nearly simultaneously, Noriega was indicted in Florida for drug trafficking and money laundering. The indictments against Noriega in Miami and Tampa began the crisis proper in Panama. Before 1988 Noriega was simply one of many dictators who had plagued Latin America and whom the United States had either tolerated or openly supported in a hemispheric anti-communism campaign. However, after

February 1988 Noriega ceased to have any benefit to U.S. foreign policy in the region and, in fact, had become a problem for the United States. His fall from favor coincided with the new U.S. policy of the "war on drugs," which defined drugs as a national security threat, supplanting the waning worldwide communism as a priority of the United States. The most tangible evidence of this shift was that Noriega was finally dropped from the CIA payroll.

Following the indictments, the United States sought to remove Noriega from power. The Reagan and Bush administrations hoped for and preferred a Panamanian solution to end Noriega's rule, such as a coup d'état or a popular uprising of the kind that removed from power dictators such as Anastasio Somoza of Nicaragua and Ferdinand Marcos of the Philippines. There was no plan, however, to remove the PDF as a political power. The first major step taken by the United States was to freeze $296 million in Panama's assets in the United States and to impose harsh economic sanctions, including the suspension of another $116 million in tax payments by U.S. companies to Panama.

Panama began a slow but steady dive into a deep economic depression. Since Panama's currency is the U.S. dollar, cash became short in supply, and by March, Noriega could not pay public employees, which caused a massive strike. But the economic crisis was mitigated for a short time when a number of Latin American and European countries came to Panama's rescue, opening up sufficient credit to allow Noriega to pay the workers.

Again, U.S. actions were actually counterproductive, since they allowed Noriega to boast of his nationalist credentials, claiming that the indictments were simply more U.S. aggression against Panama. The U.S. declarations did, however, embolden Delvalle to take action. Encouraged by the United States, on February 25 President Delvalle issued a statement that Noriega was relieved of his duties. Noriega ignored the order, claiming that Delvalle had no legal basis, which was technically correct since the 1983 amendments to the constitution stipulated that the sitting PDF commander could not be replaced by *any* president. The Noriega-controlled Legislative Assembly dismissed Delvalle and appointed a pro-Noriega man, Manuel Solís Palma, as the acting president. Washington continued to recognize Delvalle as the legitimate Panamanian president. But, having shown his hand and lost, Delvalle left Panama for exile in the United States.

However, dissatisfaction within the regime continued to mount. On March 16 Panama's chief of police, Leonidas Macías, mounted a poorly planned and, therefore, unsuccessful coup against Noriega, which the dictator used as an opportunity to consolidate his rule by seeking out other potential traitors. Despite Macías's failure, the Reagan administration continued to encourage the PDF to topple Noriega, who claimed that only two days after the failed coup he met with U.S. State Department officials William Walker and Michael Kozak, who offered to drop the drug indictments and to provide $2 million if Noriega would go into exile in Spain.[20]

After these setbacks, the U.S. State Department became the earliest proponent of using military force to remove Noriega from power in Panama. This was initially opposed by the chairman of the U.S. Joint Chiefs of Staff, Admiral William Crowe, who thought, among other things, that such a use of force would reinforce an imperialist image that would make the U.S. military presence elsewhere untenable.[21] But the PDF forced the U.S. hand.

In April 1988 U.S. troops began engaging in almost nightly firefights with PDF intruders near a fuel tank farm at Howard Air Force Base in the former Canal Zone. Amid the rising pressure, Reagan proposed one last deal for Noriega to entice him to retire, though Vice President Bush as well as some members of Congress were against any more deals. But the final deal was offered via Secretary of State Schultz with the caveat that May 25 was the deadline. Though Noriega initially accepted it at the last moment, he sought a delay to ostensibly convince other PDF officers to accept it as well. Not willing to play more games, the United States withdrew the deal and imposed encompassing economic sanctions against Panama, including a suspension of canal payments, a prohibition of U.S. citizens doing business with Panama, and the freezing of all Panamanian assets in the United States.[22]

It was hoped that Noriega's supporters and the Panamanian people would turn on him as Panama's treasury ran dry and their hardships grew. The sanctions were indeed devastating to the country, but again, inadvertently strengthened Noriega's position. Many of his fiercest opponents, such as Panama's Catholic Church and the Panamanian civilian employees of the canal, were more opposed—at least for the moment—to Washington's economically destructive tactics. Only the National Civic Crusade, which had U.S. financial support, approved of the sanctions.

To further pressure Noriega, the United States began a slow buildup of troops in the various bases along the canal, but the Panamanian leader was unfazed. At least three covert operations were planned by the United States to kidnap Noriega, but in at least one instance, a leak to the U.S. press scuttled the plan. Though having failed repeatedly in the past, for months in the last half of 1988 envoys from the Reagan administration presented multiple deals to persuade Noriega to leave quietly and with a large payoff, which was in direct contravention to the standing drug-trafficking indictments in Florida. These mixed and conflicting messages were typical of all the U.S. efforts up to this point. Interagency disagreements, turf battles, and the lack of coordination correctly gave Noriega the impression that Washington was not yet united in ousting him.

This wavering approach to military action ended with the election of George H. W. Bush as U.S. president in November 1988. Though perceived as not being as "cowboy strong" as Reagan had been, Bush was a strong supporter of the U.S. so-called "war on drugs," which gave the new U.S. president a prima facie motive to pursue his former CIA informant. However, as previously stated, Noriega's drug-trafficking activities had been common knowledge in the U.S. intelligence community for almost two decades. In fact, U.S. attorney general Edwin Meese and Drug Enforcement Agency director John Lawn had congratulated Noriega in 1987 for his "personal commitment" to fighting drug trafficking.[23] In the end, it was simply the blinding spotlight of investigative reporting by American and Panamanian journalists that finally made Noriega too embarrassing an asset for the United States to keep. The long war of words and feigned action between the United States and Panama was drawing to an end.

THE LAST STRAW

In December 1988, Bush declared unequivocally that "Noriega must go," and polls taken in Panama in late 1988 showed that a vast majority of Panamanians agreed with him. During 1988, the PDF had become ever-more brazen in its harassment of the United States: Servicemen were illegally detained and others physically assaulted, U.S. mail was stopped, and diplomatic dispatches were intercepted.

Under the U.S. sanctions, Panama's economic system had virtually shut down. All banks were closed and accounts were frozen to prevent what would have been the inevitable capital flight. Even Panama's preferential trade status with the United States was revoked. One of the last acts under the Reagan administration had been to invoke the International Emergency Economic Powers Act (a precursor to the current Helms-Burton law), legislation that banned payments to Panama by any U.S. company or citizen.

The new Bush administration hoped, perhaps against hope, that the upcoming Panamanian presidential elections on May 7 would be fair and would provide for a transition away from Noriega's rule. But, given Noriega's previous dishonesty, it was assumed by many observers in both countries that the PDF would likely try to sway the vote. The Bush administration went out of its way to express support for the Panamanian people and the PDF, sans Noriega. It was hoped that the Panamanian people or the other PDF officers would rise up and do the job for Washington. However, with the growing probability of some type of U.S. action, the opposition political parties and civic groups in Panama saw no reason to risk themselves if the United States would do the job for them.[24]

In one of his first official duties, President Bush signed a secret order that funneled $10 million in aid to Noriega's opponents for political activities leading up to the election on May 7, 1989. The amount of money in a country of 10 million is astounding when one considers that if an amount proportional to its population were introduced into a U.S. election it would be equivalent to about $1 billion.

Though assassinations of foreign leaders by the United States had been banned by executive order since 1976, the Bush administration set about changing the order's language to permit that option. This route, however, was ultimately put on hold for fear of tarnishing the U.S. image abroad if it were found complicit in the assassination of a foreign leader. But the entire plan finally fell apart after a CIA operative who was using the money to fund antigovernment radio programs was captured by Noriega's G-2, and Carlos Eleta Alamarán, the Panamanian in charge of the money distribution, was arrested on drug charges in the United States.

In the run-up to the elections, Panama's opposition called for the renewal of press freedoms, the return of exiles, and the restoration of the Electoral Tribunal. But in the end, some of the opposition did not even bother to participate in the election because of the expectation of widespread fraud, which was unfortunate given the fact that polling in late 1988 had shown that the opposition held a two-to-one advantage in public opinion.

Three main political parties participated. Noriega's pro-government coalition, a loose grouping of eight parties headed by the PRD, was called COLINA. COLINA's presidential candidate was Carlos Duque, a close business associate of Noriega. The opposition also put together a coalition, called the Democratic Opposition Civil Alliance (ADOC), composed of six different parties. But without the presence of the perennial candidate, Arnulfo Arias, who had died the previous year, the ADOC chose a wealthy businessman, Guillermo Endara, as the presidential candidate and Ricardo Arias Calderón and Guillermo "Billy" Ford for first and second vice presidents, respectively. COLINA and ADOC's political and economic platforms were remarkably similar, which meant that the election was, as Zimbalist and Weeks describe, really "a plebiscite on Noriega's rule."[25]

When the elections were concluded on May 7, 1989, the exit polls demonstrated an opposition victory, with ADOC at 73 percent and COLINA at 26 percent. The victory was endorsed by a slew of observers ranging from the Panama's Catholic Church to international election observers such as former U.S. presidents Jimmy Carter and Gerald Ford, who had all convened in Panama to try to prevent a repeat of the 1984 electoral fraud. In the face of such an overwhelming margin of victory for Endara's coalition, Noriega's forces seized ballot boxes and manipulated the returns to give victory to his candidate. The very next day COLINA published a news story proclaiming Duque the winner.

The fraud was immediately reported to the world by the press. Though Noriega tried to stop him through a brief house arrest, Jimmy Carter gave a press conference in which he famously questioned the Noriega government in his best Georgia-accented Spanish, "Are you honest people or are you thieves?" and called for a worldwide condemnation of Noriega's regime.[26] In addition, all the support that Noriega had garnered from other Latin American countries before the elections evaporated with the fraud. Noriega stood alone, and his country fell into anarchy at his feet.

The streets of Panama City erupted in protest, and the PDF and paramilitary units called "Dignity Battalions" responded with vicious abandon. When the ADOC candidates dared to lead demonstrations in protest, they were beaten and arrested in front of the international media. The bloody beating of Guillermo Ford, in particular, was captured live for a worldwide audience. Ford's pummeling at the hands of Noriega's thugs became emblematic of the lawlessness and chaos in Panama and helped galvanize U.S. public support of stronger action against Noriega. Playing his last card, Noriega nullified the election result on May 10, claiming that "the normal electoral process was altered by the obstructionist actions of a number of foreigners," naming the United States in particular. Noriega named an old high school classmate, Francisco Rodríguez, as the provisional president.

The following day, President Bush outlined a plan to remove Noriega through a combination of carrots and sticks. As the enticement, Bush proclaimed U.S. solidarity with the people of Panama and implied U.S. support of the PDF in a post-Noriega Panama, which was a clear call for a PDF coup against Noriega. The United States withdrew its ambassador, signaling a major diplomatic crisis was at hand, and the United States also initiated a large-scale military buildup at its Panama bases, sending a brigade of soldiers right through Panamanian territory to taunt the PDF.[27]

The Organization of American States (OAS) tried to mediate the crisis, but its conflicting missions—a desire to let Panama handle its own internal affairs juxtaposed with an obligation to support free elections and democracy—meant that its hands were tied. It simply issued a condemnation of the electoral fraud, which included a statement that declared that "no state . . . has the right to intervene . . . in the internal or external affairs of another," which ironically the OAS representative of the United States signed. From May to October 1989, the United States and Panama engaged in a heated and tense war of words until finally one last attempt from within Panama was made to end the standoff.

On October 3, 1989, Moisés Giraldi, an officer in Noriega's inner circle, carried out a well-planned coup attempt against Noriega. Tipped off by Giraldi's wife, the U.S. military blocked off key roads to try to prevent loyal PDF soldiers from helping Noriega. Giraldi held Noriega for hours, trying unsuccessfully to convince the dictator to step down. Then Giraldi proposed turning Noriega over to the waiting U.S. military, but his offer was inexplicably refused by the United States. During this confusion, loyal PDF forces used an air drop to bypass the U.S. military and were able to rescue Noriega. Giraldi and some of his fellow conspirators were brutally tortured and murdered by Noriega and his loyalists, and reports by the U.S. military and Panamanian human rights groups allege that between 100 and 233 of the would-be coup makers and their supporters were eventually murdered.[28]

Giraldi's failed coup attempt released all remaining restraint on Noriega's repression. Noriega's Dignity Battalions and Doberman riot police freely beat anyone considered to be even remotely dissident, all of which was frequently captured live on U.S. television screens, but not in Panama where the media was under total censorship. All the U.S. efforts to oust Noriega to this point had failed, since U.S. officials had grossly underestimated Noriega's survival skills. Bureaucratic infighting, mixed messages, and infighting between the U.S. Congress and the president had only worsened a bad situation.

The plans for a U.S. invasion were revisited after the so-called "school bus crisis." On March 3, the PDF seized over 20 U.S. school buses with children of U.S. military and civilian personnel aboard. U.S. military police intervened and defused the incident within a few hours. However, the provocation had a profound effect on the resident U.S. community in Panama, who sent a slew of messages to the U.S. Congress asking for action against the Noriega regime. A state-of-siege mentality had been established among the resident U.S. population in Panama, which added credibility to the upcoming U.S. action. Following the incident, President Bush irritably declared that "amateur hour is over."[29] Interestingly, then–U.S. secretary of defense Richard Cheney admitted to the *New York Times* that the invasion had been in planning since before the failed May election; in fact planning began in August 1988 under the codename *Blue Spoon*.

At this point the signs of imminent U.S. military action became obvious. During the summer of 1989, over 50,000 U.S. military dependents living in Panama were ordered to return to the United States, and tanks and helicopters were transported to U.S. bases in Panama, in direct violation of the canal treaties. In addition, the U.S. military conducted exercises outside the Canal Zone, also in violation of treaties.

In November 1989, the United States declared that no Panamanian registered ships could dock in U.S. ports beginning in 1990, which would drastically affect Panama, home to one of the world's largest ship registries. By December 1989 the Panamanian PDF had been on high alert for an extended period. As the old adage describes, Panama had become "not a country with an army, but an army with a country."

INVASION

On December 15, 1989, Noriega's rubber-stamp legislature gave him the title of chief executive officer of the government. Full of bravado, if not foolhardiness, Noriega declared before the Panamanian National Assembly that a "state of war existed" with the United States. But it was an incident the next day that actually lit the fuse for the U.S. invasion.

On December 16 a U.S. Marine, Robert Paz, was shot and killed in a private vehicle at a checkpoint near the PDF headquarters. The same day, a U.S. Navy lieutenant and his wife were arrested, interrogated, beaten, and tortured.[30] The following day, Secretary of Defense Dick Cheney and the chairman of the Joint Chiefs of Staff, General Powell, briefed the U.S. president on the murder. Powell recommended the use of military force to remove Noriega from power and further suggested a large-scale operation was needed to do it. On December 17 President Bush gave the order to execute the invasion, which was renamed *Operation Just Cause*.

The night before the invasion, Guillermo Endara, who had lost the presidency due to Noriega's nullification of the elections, and his two vice-presidents-to-be, Ricardo Arias Calderón and Guillermo Ford, were invited to dinner at a U.S. military base. They were informed of the impending military action, which put Endara in the awkward position of letting the United States install him as president of Panama or do nothing and have the United States impose an occupation government. Endara, Arias Calderón, and Ford were sworn into office by U.S. Army officers on a U.S. military base as the invasion began.

Shortly after midnight on December 20, the United States invaded Panama with 24,000 troops in its largest military operation up to that time since the Vietnam War. Though the PDF had 16,000 troops on paper, in fact, only 4,000 were trained combat-ready soldiers. Utilizing the latest in sophisticated modern weaponry, the U.S. invasion was completely one sided. The United States utilized overwhelming firepower that included its brand-new Stealth fighter, Apache helicopter gunships, and bunker-busting 2,000-pound bombs. Twenty-seven different sites along the Panama Canal, including Panama City and Colón, were attacked simultaneously.

A primary target of the nighttime attack was the PDF headquarters, which was located in the densely populated, poor neighborhood of Panama City called El Chorillo. Systematically, entire city blocks of El Chorillo's wooden shantytown buildings were bombed or burned to the ground. In a largely symbolic attack, the Río Hato Military School, which was founded by Torrijos, was destroyed by two of the one-ton bombs. Panamanian military resistance largely evaporated within the first 12 hours.

However, the target of the invasion, Noriega, initially escaped capture. He, along with some the officers, finally turned up on December 24, having sought refuge and sanctuary in the Vatican *nunciatura*. The U.S. military encircled the papal embassy and blasted it night and day with loud rock music. Though the action was advertised as a psychological operation to rattle Noriega, it was later revealed that its purpose was specifically to prevent the press from using parabolic microphones to hear the negotiations between U.S. General Marc Cisneros and the *nunciatura's* Monsignor Laboa. The music was turned off on December 29 only after Laboa threatened to end talks.

Finally, on January 3, 1990, after protracted discussions that included Panama's new government, the Catholic Church, and the U.S. government, Noriega, dressed in his best military uniform, emerged from the *nunciatura* and surrendered to U.S. forces. He was arrested and flown in shackles to Miami for prosecution on the drug charges. To defend its actions, the Bush administration argued that the Noriega regime threatened the safety of U.S. citizens, the integrity of the canal treaties, and the safety of the Panama Canal—a waterway that was technically still under U.S. protection. The United States bolstered its claims by using references to clauses in the UN Charter, the OAS Charter, and the Panama Canal Treaty, which all contain clauses specifying a country's right to self-defense.

However, much of the rest of the world reacted negatively. Latin America governments, even Pinochet's Chile, condemned the invasion and demanded the immediate withdrawal of U.S. forces from Panama. Most Latin American countries assumed that the United States wanted to retain some measure of control over the canal, which the destruction of Panama's military would facilitate. One day after the invasion the Organization of American States voted overwhelmingly to censure the United States, stating that it "deeply deplored" the invasion. Then, on December 29 the United Nations condemned the invasion as a "flagrant violation of international law," though a formal resolution to that effect by the UN Security Council was vetoed by the United States, Britain, and France.

As the Panamanian PDF melted away under the U.S. onslaught, so too did law and order. The aftermath of the invasion was catastrophic both to Panama's population and to its infrastructure. For two weeks after the initial invasion, utter lawlessness ruled Panama City as looters ransacked all the stores, and mobs wielding guns, bats, and crow bars prowled the streets. It is known that at least 300 Panamanian soldiers and 60 U.S. servicemen died in the conflict, but it is difficult to assess with precision the exact number of Panamanian civilians who died. The U.S. military officially estimated the death toll among Panamanian civilians at 250. However, the accuracy of this figure is in question for a number of reasons: The dead were quickly buried in at least 15 mass graves or were incinerated by the U.S. military before they could be identified. All of Panama's hospitals and morgues were put under U.S. military control and their death records sent to U.S. military bases. In the case of least one hospital, most of the doctors were arrested by U.S. forces, presumably to prevent their reports of the casualties. No independent reporters were allowed into Panama by the U.S. military until three days after the invasion, and even then they were held on military installations and given "official" information via briefings.

However, an independent study by former U.S. attorney general Ramsey Clark, which was corroborated by hundreds of testimonials given by Panamanians and reporters to the Central American Human Rights Commission and the International Red Cross, provided a conservative estimate of at least 3,000 actual civilian deaths, and some independent estimates ran much higher. In the weeks following the invasion, the U.S. military imposed a de facto state of martial law in which at least 7,000 Panamanian union and opposition party leaders were arrested and were held for days, weeks, or in some cases, months without charge.

Official U.S. estimates of the damage caused by the invasion were placed at around $2 billion. At least 20,000 Panamanians lost their homes, and post-invasion looting and vandalism were rampant. The devastated areas in El Chorillo around PDF headquarters left over 10,000 homeless and came to be called "little Hiroshima." This looting exacted ruinous losses on many Panamanian businesses, and some required many years to recover. Almost 3,000 residents of El Chorillo were later compensated $6,500 each by the United States. The next year, the U.S. Congress would approve a half billion dollar economic reconstruction package for Panama.

Nonetheless, amid the catastrophic economic damage and loss of life, a *CBS News* poll found that 80 percent of Panamanians—even those who had lost their homes or relatives—approved of the invasion. However, a similar number also did not want the United States to give up control of the canal to Panama, citing fears of Panamanian politicians using the waterway's revenues for cronyism. Amid the unprecedented destruction and death, Noriega and his dictatorship were gone, and Panama's road to recovery had begun.

NOTES

1. Graham Green, "The Country with Five Frontiers." *New York Times Review of Books* 24, no. 2 (17 February 1977): 13

2. Former Panamanian President Ernesto Pérez Balladares (1994–1999), interviewed by author, March 23, 1998.

3. John Dinges, *Our Man in Panama* (New York: Random House, 1990), 117.

4. Walter LaFeber, *The Panama Canal: The Crisis in Historical Perspective* (New York: Oxford University Press, 1989), 191.

5. David Norman Miller, "Panama and U.S. Policy," *Global Affairs* IV, no. 3 (Summer 1989): 136.

6. Victor Ostrovsky and Claire Hoy, *By Way of Deception* (New York: St. Martin's Press, 1990), 106–107.

7. Andrew Zimbalist and John Weeks, *Panama at the Crossroads: Economic Development and Political Change in the Twentieth Century* (Berkeley: University of California Press, 1991), 130–132.

8. Margaret E. Scranton, *The Noriega Years: U.S.-Panamanian Relations, 1981–1990* (Boulder, CO: Lynne Rienner Publishers, 1991), 87.

9. Edward F. Dolan, *Panama and the United States: Their Canal, Their Stormy Years* (New York: Franklin Watts, 1990), 132.

10. Eytan Gilboa, "The Panama Invasion Revisited: Lessons for the Use of Force in the Post Cold War Era," *Political Science Quarterly* 110, no. 4 (1995): 539.

11. Kevin Buckley, *Panama: The Whole Story* (New York: Simon & Schuster, 1991), 46

12. Peter M. Sánchez, "The End of Hegemony? Panama, the United States and Latin American Security After the Year 2000," presented at the Latin American Studies Association Conference, Chicago, IL, 1998.

13. Michael Conniff, *Panama and the United States: The Forced Alliance* (Athens, GA: University of Georgia Press, 1992), 155.

14. *La Prensa* (Panama City), July 12, 1986.

15. R. M. Koster and Guillermo Sánchez, *In the Time of Tyrants: Panama, 1968–1990* (New York: W. W. Norton, 1990), 336.

16. Steve C. Ropp, "Explaining the Long-Term Maintenance of a Military Regime: Panama before the U.S. Invasion." *World Politics* 44, no. 2 (January 1992): 228

17. Margaret Scranton, "The Civic Crusade in Panama: Contributions and Limitations of Nonviolent Action against a Dictatorship." (paper presented at the Harvard Seminar on Nonviolent Sanctions and Cultural Survival, Cambridge, MA, spring 1992).

18. Andrew Zimbalist and John Weeks, *Panama at the Crossroads* (Berkeley: University of California Press, 1991), 146.

19. Michael Conniff: 157.

20. Peter Eisner, *America's Prisoner: The Memoirs of Manuel Noriega* (New York: Random House, 1997), 224.

21. Frederick Kempe, *Divorcing the Dictator: America's Bungled Affair with Noriega* (New York: G. P. Putnam, 1990), 297.

22. Margaret Scranton, *The Noriega Years* (Boulder, CO: Westview Press, 1991), 132–140

23. *Los Angeles Times*, January 16, 1990.

24. Former Panamanian President Ernesto Pérez Balladares (1994–1999), interviewed by author, 1997.

25. Zimbalist and Weeks, 152.

26. Jimmy Carter, "Free Elections Are Only the Beginning," *Foreign Service Journal* (February 2001): 4.

27. Margaret E. Scranton, 165.

28. *Washington Post*, November 22, 1989.

29. Robert Woodward, *The Commanders*, (New York: Simon & Schuster, 1991), 127–128.

30. Thomas Donnelly, et al., *Operation Just Cause* (New York: Lexington Books, 1991), 92–93.

7

Democracy and the Canal Gained

In John Le Carré's *The Tailor of Panama*, a character quips, "When [George H. W.] Bush came in and removed Ali Baba [Noriega], he left the 40 thieves." Though the invasion did remove Noriega, destroy the PDF, and install a legitimately elected president, Guillermo Endara, it did not immediately change many of the problems underlying Panamanian society.

Though for the first time since 1968 a purely civilian government was in power, the issues of power and legitimacy were far from resolved. For one, Endara's administration was viewed as an implementer of U.S. policy and therefore enjoyed little legitimacy in the eyes of many Panamanians. The country was still mired in catastrophic debt and the impending assumption of the Panama Canal was clouded by continued political polarization, charges of cronyism, and the increased penetration of drug trafficking and drug money into the Panamanian economy.

Panama's move toward civilian leadership necessitated the construction of democratic institutions and reforms to its electoral system. Endara took office pledging to foster Panama's economic recovery, reform the Panamanian military as an apolitical force under civilian control, and strengthen the country's nascent democratic institutions. Panama's Electoral Tribunal conducted an election recount based on copies of the results of the 1989 elections, which had been safeguarded by the papal *nunciatura* (where Noriega had sought refuge), and a new National Assembly was installed. Renamed the Legislative Assembly, it quickly repealed all the Noriega-era decrees that had eliminated the freedom of speech and assembly.[1]

RIGHTING THE SHIP OF STATE

As the gravest problem, the economy deservedly received the most immediate attention. After years of economic sanctions as well as the destruction and looting following the U.S. invasion, the amount of economic aid needed to rebuild Panama's tattered economy was estimated at more than $2 billion. But the Bush administration promised only half that amount, which was further reduced to $420 million by the U.S. Congress. In addition, the United States turned over only 35 percent of the $400 million it had frozen during the last two years of the Noriega dictatorship.

Unemployment, which had been estimated at 20 percent prior to the invasion, rose to over 30 percent in its aftermath. The miserable conditions were exacerbated by structural adjustment conditions placed upon the aid by the U.S. Agency for International Development, which included the encouragement of beef and corn exports to the United States and a reduction of public services utilized by Panama's poor majority. Ironically, after the implementation of U.S. economic assistance, unemployment rose again to encompass one-half of all Panamanians.

After a slow start caused by this chronic lack of finance, the Endara government slowly started to put the country back on its economic feet, but this early democratic period was fairly chaotic politically, as Endara enjoyed little legitimacy. His weakness rested partly on the fact that his political party, the Partido Arnulfista, had a very small base, and that most cabinet positions were held by the parties of his two vice presidents, Guillermo Ford and Ricardo Arias Calderón, who were jockeying—as was traditional in Panamanian politicians—for position to reap the rewards of political power. In sharp contrast to the Torrijos-Noriega period, where political posts had been occupied by various ethnicities, especially mestizos, the Endara government revived the pre-1968 *rabiblanco* tradition of practically all ministerial positions being held by whites. This exclusion only increased the antagonism and resentment felt among the remnants of the defeated PDF forces, who were largely mestizo. The majority of the new police force was composed of former, mostly mestizo, PDF members. This tension was so high that Endara was able to stay in office only because U.S. troops remained to counter a PDF rebellion.

But even the U.S. presence was not sufficient to mollify the boiling cauldron of discontent. Almost one year after the U.S. invasion hobbled the PDF, on December 4, 1990, former Panamanian military officers—now designated as police officers—broke their jailed leader, Eduardo Herrera, out of jail in a bold helicopter raid. They were joined in the rebellion by 100 former soldiers, creating a situation that threatened to break apart the fragile bonds that held together the Endara government. Only the intervention of the U.S. military the following day restored order. Although quickly put down by U.S. military forces, the uprising revealed the weakness of the strategy of using former PDF members in the police force.[2] Not until the following year was the U.S. military able to withdraw its forces from Panama.

To quash further uprisings, Endara's government proposed a number of measures. First, the military officer corps was purged of all remaining PDF loyalists. Second, a law was passed that gave the police its first civilian commander-in-chief since 1930. Finally, in a sweeping move, a constitutional amendment was proposed that would make Panama the second Latin American country (after Costa Rica) to abolish its military. The amendment was approved in October 1994 by the Legislative Assembly. In the PDF's place, a new security institution was established called the Public Force (PF), which divided up security responsibilities into four different areas. However, a "back door" was created in the amendment to permit the formation of temporary special police units to counter acts of "external aggression."

Though Endara himself was favored by U.S. policymakers, his reforms did not soothe the fears of some U.S. lawmakers who anxiously, even fearfully, saw the turnover of the canal as a foreign policy disaster. Some U.S. policymakers called for a new treaty that would allow the United States to maintain troops in Panama beyond 1999. Multiple resolutions were made in the U.S. Congress, but none came to fruition. Even from the Panamanian side overtures were made to maintain a U.S. presence. A Panamanian delegation came to Washington to explore the possibility of renegotiation of the troop withdrawal agreement, but came up empty-handed. In the end, neither side was willing to make sufficient concessions to reverse what Torrijos and Carter had created.

The reason for the Panamanians' trepidation was principally economic. Prior to the 1990s the U.S. military personnel's spending in Panama contributed around 5 percent of Panama's GDP, and around 75,000 Panamanians depended on income from the bases and businesses serving the bases. There was also widespread doubt among common Panamanians that their government would be able to resist the temptation of using former U.S. properties, including prime real estate in Panama City and throughout the former Canal Zone, as cannon fodder in a stealth war of crony capitalism.

There was plenty of precedent to support these misgivings. The critics based their predictions on the example of the Panama Railroad and other properties turned over to Panama by the United States in 1979 as the first step in the Panama Canal treaties. After getting the railroad, the Torrijos government had quintupled the employee roster to bolster its public image but practically eliminated the maintenance budget.[3] By the early 1990s, the railroad had deteriorated so much that it was largely unusable. Additionally, former U.S. canal administration buildings that had been handed over had been ransacked and become squatter homes.

EXORCIZING GHOSTS

In April 1991, President Endara set up an 11-member commission to study the best way to utilize the U.S. bases, but it fell short of its goal as every sector of the government intransigently maneuvered for its own piece of the canal pie. In 1992, as part of the democratic project, Panama's courts convicted Noriega en absentia for orchestrating the murder of Hugo Spadafora. But no lasting effort was made to have him extradited from the United States where his true fate lay.

In the same year in Miami, Noriega was tried and convicted on eight counts of drug trafficking, racketeering, and money laundering. The trial was rife with irregularities, such as cash payments to witnesses in return for testimony against Noriega. In the end, Noriega was sentenced to 40 years in prison (his sentence was subsequently reduced to 30 years). In later years, numerous federal agents with intimate knowledge of drug trafficking in the region testified that the charges were trumped up.

The one bright point during this period was the decision regarding the canal's future. The so-called "Tripartite Commission," originally formed in 1986 by Japan, Panama, and the United States, had been studying alternatives to Panama. In September 1993 its study concluded that if the Gaillard Cut (the narrowest part of the canal) were widened, the canal could handle shipping requirements until the year 2020, thus negating the need for a second sea-level canal, which would cost over $20 billion. This project would occupy Panama for the coming decade.

Economically, Panama was able to overcome these early hurdles. A combination of capital inflows and private consumption helped the economy grow at a respectable rate of 4 percent. During Endara's administration, urban poverty was reduced, but the wealth gap remained largely unresolved. Despite some good news, these modest gains did not mollify the Panamanian public's disapproval of the government and protests against it. In response, Endara, in a twist of irony to his purported democratic goals, increasingly used the police to suppress public dissent, which further damaged the government's credibility. Endara had entered the presidency with a 70 percent approval rating, but by May 1992 only 10 percent of Panamanians supported him.[4]

Amid the mostly negative news, the beleaguered president responded to his political isolation by reverting to the Panamanian traditions of nepotism and authoritarianism, hiring former business partners as ministers to fortify his cabinet with loyalists. His administration imploded as First Vice President Calderón resigned, five of his cabinet ministers were fired, and several assassination plots against Endara were uncovered. Endara's fledgling democratic government faced the daunting task of trying to begin the process of democratic institutionalization within a country where none had existed before and to legitimize the government by instilling a sense of empowerment to an electorate that traditionally had very little input regarding the policies of its government.

In 1992, Panama's first nationwide vote since the invasion was held. Rather than write a new constitution, for the two years following the invasion, Panama's Legislative Assembly had debated over a mind-boggling number of amendments, including greater autonomy for various branches of government and human rights guarantees. The Endara government brought the matter before the Panamanian people in a national referendum, which was considered by many as the first credible national vote held in the country in 60 years.

Though the referendum's purpose was laudable—to reduce the power of the executive branch and to increase the separation of powers—its ultimate defeat was emblematic of Endara's troubles. It was rejected by a margin of two to one and almost 60 percent of the electorate abstained, many saying that it had become too cumbersome to understand. But the defeat had a silver lining. The referendum vote had been open and transparent and helped contribute to building democratic practices in Panama.[5]

For all the troubles that plagued his tenure, the work of the Endara's administration did begin to help to build Panama's democratic institutions, principally by strengthening the independence of various branches of government and, perhaps most important, the Electoral Tribunal, which in 1994 was to oversee the first postinvasion presidential election.

A BULL IN THE CANAL

Change augured in the 1994 presidential election, which was the first completely free election since 1968 and most certainly the freest ever held in Panama up to that date.[6] Four and half years after the U.S. invasion, the PRD was again challenging for the presidency, though now as a strictly civilian party. Capitalizing upon Endara's image of ineptness and illegitimacy, the PRD's candidate was the former secretary general of the PRD, Ernesto Pérez Balladares, who was part of a three-party center-left coalition called Pueblo Unido (People United).

Considered by many to be Torrijos's prótegé, Pérez Balladares criticized Endara's government for corruption and touted the PRD's populist past. Even so, some Panamanians remained cautious of the PRD's return to political power, fearing that it could signify a return to the authoritarianism and corruption that characterized the military government's years in power. But Pérez Balladares competently eased fears—both at home and in the United States—by promising to fight narco-trafficking and maintain civilian leadership of the nation's security forces. This helps to explain the lack of U.S. interest in the elections since, for the first time in many decades, the United States did not openly favor any candidate. The primary competition was Arnulfo Arias's widow, Mireya Moscoso of the Partido Arnulfista, and a new addition to the usual political contenders, world-famous Panamanian salsa singer Rubén Blades, who headed a new party called Papá Egoró ("Mother Earth" in an indigenous Panamanian language), which would receive more votes than any other pre-1990 civilian party except the Arnulfistas.

In the end, Pérez Balladares edged out Moscoso and Blades, but his victory was bittersweet. He only received 33 percent of the vote in a field of six candidates, which left him without a mandate. On the other hand, with the support of allied parties, the PRD achieved an effective majority in the Legislative Assembly. Although the usual unfair Panamanian practice of the sitting president using state funds for his campaign had occurred, the most important upshot of this election was that it was very "Costa Rican" in its outcome.[7] Once the result was announced, the losers graciously accepted defeat without the previous consternation, and Pérez Balladares assumed the presidency without incident on September 1, 1994.

Nicknamed "Toro" (Bull) because of his imposing physical stature, Pérez Balladares fit well the mold of previous *rabiblanco* presidents of Panama, despite his *torrijista* pedigree. The son of a Nicaraguan immigrant doctor, Pérez Balladares had been educated in the United States, earning an MBA from the University of Notre Dame. He created controversy within his party when he broke with political tradition and appointed members of other parties to about one-third of his cabinet positions. While it had the practical effect of reducing in-fighting, this conciliatory gesture was importantly recognized as setting the tone for reconciliation and compromise that promised to strengthen the political system's democratic foundations.[8]

Pérez Balladares entered the presidency with the same stellar approval ratings Endara had enjoyed at the beginning. But the Panama that Pérez Balladares inherited was still troubled and burdened with the second-highest foreign debt in Central America. Though Endara's administration had begun to pay down the debt, it still remained critically high at $2,600 per capita in a country where the GDP per capita was $2,256. Likewise Panama's population still suffered from widespread poverty and unemployment—over one-third of Panamanians were poor.

The problem was both structural and historic. Without a doubt, the Noriega-era sanctions by the United States and associated negative factors had damaged the economy. But by the 1990s, Panama had a solidly "dual economy," in which a very small sector—banking, trade, and services—produced the greatest proportion of the GDP. This sector employed only about 3 percent of Panama's workforce and was concentrated almost exclusively around Panama City. The remainder of Panama's workers labored in the less lucrative areas, such as agriculture, and most postinvasion economic programs were not agricultural in nature.

Pérez Balladares liked to call his approach to reforming Panama "renovated *Torrijismo*," after the former dictator's neo-socialist policies. Most of the new president's early programs were focused on reducing crime, which had been critically high since the invasion, and on implementing tightened control measures on business to reduce money laundering, corruption, and tax evasion.

However, in practice Pérez Balladares was less socialist in policymaking than was his mentor. As a millionaire businessman, his economics were firmly rooted in orthodox free market policies, which necessitated neoliberal cost-cutting measures that angered many Panamanian workers. His policies resulted in growth for some select slices of the economy, but for the majority of Panamanians the trend was toward greater unemployment, underemployment, and higher prices.

For example, labor rights were diluted in 1995 when Pérez Balladares pushed labor code revisions through the Legislative Assembly. These changes brought Panamanians back into the streets in protest and the government reciprocated with repression. When 49 unions initiated peaceful protests against the revisions, the government cracked down in a series of violent clashes, resulting in four deaths and hundreds of arrests. The popularity of the government declined accordingly.

An important part of the economic reform package was the government's privatization program. One of its most important public goods, the port system, was put up for sale. A Hong Kong-based Chinese company, Hutchinson Whampoa, won the contract from the Panamanian government in 1995 to operate the ports of Balboa, near the Pacific entry to the Panama Canal, and Cristóbal, on the Atlantic side. The world's largest port company, Hutchinson Whampoa subsequently spent over $100 million in renovations, giving Panama some of the world's most modern ports. Prominent members of the U.S. Congress complained that the decision was a security threat to the United States and that the Chinese company could deny passage to U.S. vessels, even though Panama's constitution guarantees the canal's neutrality and places the waterway under the Panamanian government's direct authority.

The real problems for Pérez Balladares began, ironically, in an area he had pledged to reform—drug trafficking. During his campaign for president, he had promised to eliminate drug trafficking, and to aid this endeavor the United States had given Panama over $3 million in aid to create an anti-trafficking police force. But in January 1996 an investigation by Panama's banking commission found that the Agro-Industrial and Commercial Bank of Panama (BANAICO) had been used as a major drug-money laundering center for the Colombian Cali Cartel. Unwittingly or not, Pérez Balladares's campaign had accepted drug money from the cartel's number-one man in Panama, José Castrillón Henao, who later detailed his transactions after having been extradited from a Panamanian prison to the United States to stand trial on charges of money laundering. Though drug trafficking had taken on great importance in the U.S. relationship with Panama, the United States was reluctant to press the issue since it was still hoping to negotiate a deal to keep 2,000 U.S. troops in Panama after the Panama Canal and all its bases revert to Panamanian control in 1999.

The U.S. officials were not alone in their reluctance to see U.S. troops leave. Many Panamanians did not want the United States to leave. In a poll taken in Panama in 1996, 78 percent of Panamanians surveyed expressed a hope that the U.S. military would remain in some capacity. Part of the fear was based on the economic losses. The U.S. military annually put $350 million into Panama's economy and, in addition, United States directly employed 2,800 local civilians in a variety of jobs. The salaries of Panamanian workers in the Canal Zone, such as plumbers, were greater than those of Panamanian professionals outside the zone, such as doctors.

The other reason Panamanians wanted a continued U.S. presence was the fear that without the tempering presence of the United States, Panamanian politicians would turn the country into a personal wealth-creation vehicle.

Hoping to mold the U.S. opinion of him, Pérez Balladares, as a gesture of cooperation with Washington, agreed to allow the United States to settle as many as 10,000 Cuban refugees of the 1994 "Balsero Crisis" on its military bases in the Panama Canal area. This did not prove as controversial as his decision to grant amnesty to former employees of the Noriega regime, some of whom had been in prison since the U.S. invasion. The measure was opposed by most non-PRD deputies, including the Solidarity Party members needed to make up the PRD's governing majority, which amounted to only 32 seats in the 71-member Assembly. Once again, Panamanian politics and society were split down the middle in partisan camps.

But, in the end, the wheels of change were unstoppable, and in 1997 Miami lured the Panama Canal-based U.S. Southern Command, the U.S. military's headquarters for security operation in Latin America. Other U.S. military operations were transferred elsewhere in Latin America. By the time the turnover point would arrive, the United States would have essentially abandoned all its facilities to Panama's authorities.

ECHOES OF THE PAST

Despite his promises and effort, Pérez Balladares had a difficult time casting off his party's authoritarian past. A significant step toward the institutionalization of Panama's young democracy occurred in 1998 through the demonstration of Pérez Balladares's ominous intolerance of criticism and dissent. In January 1998, the government charged Gustavo Gorriti, a Peruvian journalist who worked for the ever-critical Panamanian daily *La Prensa*, with slander of the attorney general.

The allegation was based on the *ley mordaza* (gag law), a set of restrictions that had been used under the previous dictatorships to curtail freedom of the press, close newspapers, and silence reporters. The law permitted reporters to be punished for publishing anything that reputedly damaged the nation's economy or its national security, and the parameters of such an infraction were essentially at the discretion of the chief executive. Pérez Balladares availed himself of the law with greater frequency in his last year in office. The action came only four months after the government dropped its two-month effort to deport Gorriti, who headed *La Prensa's* investigative unit, which had conducted the probe that proved a Colombian drug cartel had contributed over $50,000 to Pérez Balladares's election campaign. Gorriti also presented numerous charges of nepotism by the president.

In many other ways Pérez Balladares tarnished his image among Panamanians. Amid the country's continued poverty and high debt, he doubled the salaries of his cabinet members and other appointed high officials and awarded a reported $35 million in back pay to former members of Noriega's Dignity Battalions. Additionally, the son of a prominent PRD politician and two other Panamanians were exonerated of the murder of an unarmed U.S. soldier in 1992 in a trial that was plagued by political pressure and irregularities emanating from the president's office.

PANAMANIANS FIND A VOICE

If Pérez Balladares was finding the going tough up to this point, it would only get worse. The president proposed a constitutional amendment that would allow Panamanian presidents to run for a second consecutive term, which was constitutionally prohibited. However, he requested that the measure be made effective immediately so that he could run for reelection. In essence, he hoped for another five-year term so that he could be the president to accept the U.S. handover of the canal. The transparency of the request was not lost on the Panamanian public.

The amendment was resoundingly defeated in an August 1998 referendum in which almost two-thirds rejected the proposal and 34 percent of the electorate abstained. Few feared his Torrijos-related past or thought it would lead to less democracy. It was broadly understood that the defeat had dual symbolism: rejection of the reelection proposal and a symbolic repudiation of Pérez Balladares's neoliberal social and economic policies, such as the government's privatization program that allowed the sale of the state telephone system, privatization of some pension funds, and the loss of labor gains under Torrijos. According to Panamanian sociologist Marcos Gandásegui, while Panama's economy continued to grow at about 4 percent annually, the totality of the president's programs resulted in a large-scale wealth transfer from the poorest Panamanians to the wealthiest.[9]

Pérez Balladares shrugged off the defeat, claiming that it proved democracy is alive in Panama. But while he had entered office as a reformer, Pérez Balladares would leave a discredited, if not reviled, leader whose administration, much like Endara's, had become increasingly entangled in censorship, coercion, and corruption and had an increasingly tenuous claim to fidelity of the rule of law.

The only thing left to do was prepare for the transfer of the canal the following year. But even here, Pérez Balladares created controversy. A new organization was created, the Panama Canal Authority, to manage the waterway. But, its board of directors was chock-full of bankers and investment lawyers and the land inside the former Canal Zone was sold off to the highest bidders in a *"piñata"* sale, much as occurred the previous decade in Nicaragua after the fall of the Sandinistas.

A Number of Firsts

For the 1999 elections, Mireya Elisa Moscoso Rodríguez, the widow of Arnulfo Arias who had made an unsuccessful bid for the presidency in 1994, was chosen as the candidate for her husband's eponymous Partido Arnulfista (PA). The PA formed part of a conservative three-party alliance called Alianza Democrática (Democratic Alliance). Her popularity among the masses rested in the mere fact that she was the opposition. Moscoso, a teacher's daughter and former hairdresser, had never held elected office. She had married Arias when she was 23 years old and he was 67 years old while they were both in exile in Miami after Arias's last ousting at the hands of the military.

Opposing her candidacy was Martín Torrijos, son of the former dictator. Torrijos, a political novice and recently elected secretary general of the PRD (replacing Pérez Balladares in that position), was selected as the party's candidate less than six months before the election. The young Torrijos was expected to energize the party's populist base, which Pérez Balladares's neoliberal policies had alienated. Torrijos fronted a left-wing alliance of parties called Pueblo Unido (People United).

Nonetheless, Panamanians, tired of the ongoing scandals, corruption, and neoliberal economic concessions under the PRD and Pérez Balladares, handed power back to the conservatives. On May 2, 31 years after her husband was last overthrown by the Panamanian military, Moscoso became Panama's first female president. Though she handed the PRD a defeat by winning with a respectable 45 percent of the popular vote to Torrijos's 37 percent, her victory was tempered by the fact that the PRD maintained firm control of the Legislative Assembly with 46 percent of the 72 seats to the PA's 15 percent. Though some skeptics had earlier predicted that the PRD would not relinquish power, the smooth transition was proof positive that Panama's democracy was becoming institutionalized.

As Panama's first female president, Moscoso had popular opinion and history behind her. In her victory speech before 25,000 supporters in

Panama's national stadium, she pledged to eradicate social injustice and poverty. She also promised to review and possibly reverse some of the policies begun under Pérez Balladares, including the privatization of Panamanian state industries.

Moscoso's election signaled the reversal of the decidedly neoliberal policies of the latter years of Pérez Balladares's administration, and a return to the populist roots of the Arnulfistas. But Moscoso's ability to enact reform during the first year of her administration was handicapped by PRD intransigence even before the beginning of her term. She was given practically no cooperation from the outgoing Pérez Balladares administration, resulting in quid pro quo bickering in the days surrounding the transfer of power. Second, in the final days of his presidency, Pérez Balladares rushed through legislation to pack the Supreme Court with his supporters and remove presidential control of some discretionary funds.

This petty bickering aside, Moscoso's promises were aided by her inheriting a country in better shape financially than most of its neighbors. Far removed from the previous decade, economic growth was sustained at a respectable 4 percent and buoyed by over $2 billion in new investments and $4 billion in real estate that Panama would inherit with the Panama Canal. However, Moscoso conversely set the stage for worsening the economy with plans to raise protectionist agricultural tariffs and end the privatization process, which would make it more difficult for the government to secure loans from international financial institutions like the World Bank.

Most importantly, she promised a smooth handover of the Panama Canal at the end of the year and vowed to protect the waterway. But behind the scenes, Panama's new government tried one last time to convince the United States to rethink its pullout and leave some type of military force. The United States declined the offer, since its military operations that were formerly based in Panama had already been relocated, primarily to Honduras, Ecuador, Antigua, Peru, Colombia, and the Bahamas.

The Panamanian government's hesitation before full assumption of the canal was caused by the new security challenges that had arisen. The country's porous and poorly defended Darién region bordering Colombia had become the site of numerous incursions by Colombian drug traffickers and guerrilla fighters. The United States did, however, use its Special Forces to give military training to more than 350 of Panama's 11,000-member police force to help in the fight against drug trafficking in the Darién region. Beginning in 1996, Panamanian police began a vigorous program of patrolling and deporting Colombian intruders, though these countermeasures were met with criticism by world human-rights groups since some of the deportees were sent back to near-certain death at the hands of right-wing death squads in Colombia.[10]

A Virtual Minefield

Another important source of discord prior to the handover was the environmental situation in the former Canal Zone, which remains littered with lethal debris from which Panamanians are still dying. Since World War II, the U.S. military used the relative isolation afforded by its bases within the Canal Zone for a variety of arms testing. The so-called "Empire Range" was used for everything from bombing runs in the 1950s to the testing of chemical and biological agents in later decades.

Upon leaving Panama, the U.S. military left behind over 17,000 contaminated sites containing unexploded munitions throughout the canal. One test area alone—the Balboa West Range—contained more than 50,000 pieces of unexploded ordinance. In addition to explosives, numerous contaminants such as solvents to clean airplanes, petrochemicals, and PCBs have contaminated the soil and groundwater. The U.S. military routinely used pesticides that are banned in the United States to kill termites around their Panamanian bases. As of the turnover, the potable water around the canal contained over 300 percent more lead (51 parts per billion) than is deemed safe for human consumption. During the Vietnam War era, Agent Orange was tested on the forests of the Canal Zone and on San José Island in the Bay of Panama, and the Army Tropic Test Center was used as a testing site for chemical weapons such as the VX nerve agent. In total, about 3,000 hectares of Panama's land was left contaminated and unusable.

President Moscoso complained bitterly that the United States had cleaned up "practically nothing." The Panamanian Foreign Ministry filed a formal complaint against the United States and even hired a Washington, D.C., law firm to file suit against the United States, since the Panama Canal treaties required the United States to remove "every hazard to human life, health and safety" from the military areas, "insofar as may be practicable." Although the treaties required the United States to consult with Panama on environmental problems, the Pentagon did not do so, since it did not consider unexploded munitions to be toxic waste. However, depleted uranium (the chief cause of "Gulf War Syndrome"), which is used as tank armor and for armor-piercing shells, litters the former test ranges.

Some 70,000 poor Panamanians continue to live in communities that border these contaminated minefields, and at least 21 were killed and another 83 wounded during the 1990s by venturing into ordinance-littered zones.[11] The U.S. Department of Defense said that full removal of the unexploded munitions would be too costly, take at least 15 years to complete, and possibly damage the rainforest that sustains the canal. But even some U.S. officials admit that the United States did "as little as it could get away with."[12]

A Panamanian Canal

The presence of the United States, in one form or another, was omnipresent in Panamanian society throughout the twentieth century. And while the direct influence of the United States upon Panama waned somewhat during the military dictatorship, the invasion brought about a change in attitude on both sides.

As the turnover neared, the Panamanians' traditional anti-American sentiments and nationalism had been replaced by an overt strong desire that the United States remain in some capacity. In almost 30 surveys conducted from 1991 to 1999, public opinion had run as high as 76 percent for some continued American presence in Panama after 2000, even though about the same percentage had wished the Americans to leave twenty years prior. As Orlando Pérez has noted, approval for some type of U.S. presence was favored less by the elites, whose national pride precludes serious consideration of a continued U.S. presence, than by the masses, who had largely been the receiver of U.S. wages and benefits.[13]

The month leading up to the turnover of the Panama Canal was full of symbolism. On December 6, 1999, Corozal, the last U.S. military base in the country, was turned over to Panama, and eight days later a symbolic handover of the canal was conducted by former U.S. president Jimmy Carter, in a ceremony attended by six Latin American presidents. Despite the obvious frustration among conservatives in the U.S. Congress at the unusual occurrence of giving up territory to a foreign government, the United States left on schedule, but not without recrimination.

At noon on December, 31, 1999, the North American epoch in Panama came to an end. With former U.S. president and canal treaties signatory Jimmy Carter in attendance, the keys to the Panama Canal were handed over President Moscoso. Neither President Bill Clinton nor any U.S. current high official attended. In addition to the canal itself, the United States also contributed $160 million to Panama, which came from toll increases levied since 1997. The money was earmarked for long-term improvements to the canal, but many Panamanians were fearful that Moscoso's cash-strapped government would use it instead for short-term social spending.

While the official departure of the United States evoked mixed emotions among Panamanians, but there was little time for remorse. Soon the Moscoso government was forced to address a string of violent street protests against government corruption and mismanagement of the country's social security fund.

PANAMA IN THE TWENTY-FIRST CENTURY

With the transfer of the Panama Canal completed, Panamanians turned their attention to binding old wounds and firming up its young democracy. Spurred by the discovery in 1999 of what were thought to be Héctor Gallego's remains on a former Panamanian military base (Los Pumas de Tocumén) near the international airport, President Moscoso established a truth commission in December 2000 to investigate this and other gravesites. Though DNA analysis determined the bones were not Gallego's, the investigation continued, even amid death threats to the investigators.

Despite resistance by the PRD party, by April 2002 the commission had found 36 more graves at 24 different military sites and concluded that the military had engaged in inhuman and cruel torture of prisoners during the years of dictatorship. Three former military officers, Nivaldo Madriñán, Melbourne Walker, and Eugenio Mangallán had been convicted of Gallego's disappearance in 1993 and received 15-year prison sentences. In April 2002, the commission released a report that documented 110 cases of political murder and forced disappearance carried out by the Panamanian military between 1968 and 1989.

PANAMA FLIES SOLO

The Panama Canal is still important to international shipping, and every year 14,000 ships pass through it, carrying more than 4 percent of the world's trade. Former U.S. military facilities have been swiftly transformed. The former U.S. Albrook Air Force Base has become Panama City's domestic airport, and the former School of the Americas has been rebuilt as a luxury hotel and conference center. Fort Clayton, with its rolling lawns and red-tile-roofed buildings, reopened in 1999 as an education and high-technology center called the "City of Knowledge." An additional improvement, a second bridge called the "Centennial Bridge," was completed in 2004 close to the Pedro Miguel locks, 22 kilometers from Panama City.

Panama continued to face an economic shortfall. Moscoso raised taxes, but it was not sufficient to make up for the more than $1 billion she gave to Hutchison Whampoa in tax breaks. Real per capita GDP remained stagnant during her administration. Even facing increasing protests of government corruption, Moscoso's government was unable to improve

economic growth or seriously reduce corruption. However, she did win
international favor after promising to make Panama's tax system more
transparent, which got the country removed from an international list of
uncooperative tax havens. Still, for the average Panamanian, relatively
high unemployment continued to be the main worry. Officially, 16 percent
remained out of work, and underemployment was estimated to be twice
that number. Poverty levels remained high at 37 percent.

The ongoing civil war in neighboring Colombia remained a pressing
security concern. Colombia's two leftist guerrilla groups with over 20,000
men under arms—FARC (Revolutionary Armed Forced of Colombia) and
ELN (Army of National Liberation)—as well as right-wing paramilitary
forces repeatedly made incursions into Panama's Darién region, raising
concerning of a expansion of Colombia's civil war into Panama. On numerous occasions throughout the early 2000s Colombian guerrillas and
Panamanian police fought sporadically battles along the border. One of
the most affected groups was Panama's indigenous people who still live
in the Darién province bordering Colombia. In October 2003, the *Coordi-
nadora Nacional de Pueblos Indígenas de Panama* warned that indigenous
people in the Darién region were victimized by armed groups active
around the border.

Despite its official departure, the U.S. government remained very interested in Panama because of unabated drug trafficking. Colombian coca
cultivation had increased by 28 percent in the late 1990s, and virtually all
the increase occurred in areas under guerrilla or paramilitary control, including the border region with Panama. Economically, Panama still endured periodic social upheavals, such as in September 2003 when a
national strike occurred over the management of the social security fund.
Most public services were paralyzed and more than 40 persons were hurt
in clashes with the police.

Swinging the Pendulum Again

The trend of Panamanian voter wrath toward incumbents remained
constant. Preparations began early for the May 2004 election, and public
sentiment toward the incumbent Conservative Party was generally poor.
Once again Martín Torrijos was the PRD's candidate and former president
Guillermo Endara had returned for the Arnulfistas. The outgoing Moscoso
government's very poor poll numbers were evidence of the public's mood
for yet another swing in the political spectrum. Many cited the alarming
rise in violent crime during the Moscoso administration as the source of
their discontent. In a coalition with the Partido Popular, Torrijos headed

an alliance called Patria Nueva (New Homeland) that easily defeated Endara, receiving 47 percent to 30 percent, respectively. Concurrently, the PRD was swept into a legislative majority in the Legislative Assembly. For the first time since before the invasion, the leftist PRD solidly held both branches of government.

Inaugurated on September 1, 2004, Torrijos was not a carbon copy of his populist father. Though born in Panama in 1963, Torrijos had moved to the United States as a teenager and was educated there. He earned degrees in economics and political science from the University of Texas at Austin, and to fund his education had managed a branch of McDonald's in Chicago. Upon returning to Panama, he had served as deputy minister for the interior and justice under President Pérez Balladares, but Torrijos arrived in office espousing a much more market-oriented economics and "zero-tolerance" anti-corruption policy. This second successful post-independent presidential election, coupled with vastly increased civil liberties, solidified Panama's rating as one of the three freest countries in Latin America (behind Chile and Costa Rica) according to the prestigious Freedom House organization.[14]

Torrijos inherited an even more financially sound Panama. Only months after his taking office, in November 2004, it was reported that the Panama Canal earned record revenues of over $1 billion for that fiscal year. But Panama's continued foreign debt, estimated in late 2004 at almost $9 billion, brought about plans in May 2005 to increase pension contributions by individuals and raise the retirement age from 60 to 65 for men and from 57 to 62 for women. In response, in July 2005, Panamanians took to the streets in weeks of protests and strikes, including the closure of the University of Panama by its students in solidarity with workers. President Torrijos had promised to reform the cash-strapped social security system. But Torrijos was forced to shelve these plans after they met with stiff resistance from unions and the Catholic Church. The Torrijos government claimed that the system was heading for bankruptcy but, again, most Panamanians say corruption is at the heart of the shortages. The proposal to increase the retirement age was postponed until perhaps 2006. The year 2005 closed with a record 14,011 vessels traversing the Panama Canal, up 4.6 percent from the previous year.

LOOKING FORWARD THROUGH THE PAST

The modern state of Panama has been strongly influenced by almost 150 years of U.S. presence, investment, and intervention. Though fully independent today, in many ways Panama remains an enduring testament to its U.S. heritage. It is virtually the only Latin American country where baseball (with due apologies to Cuba and the Dominican Republic) and basketball trump soccer as favorite sports and where Halloween, Thanksgiving, and Valentine's Day are celebrated. Many in Panama agree that there has been tendency in practically all sectors of Panamanian society to assume that the United States would solve any problem in Panama. That attitude is undoubtedly one of the country's greatest societal hurdles.

Along with most of Latin America, Panama has steadily faded from the list of priorities of U.S. policymakers. The removal of the U.S. military's command center for Latin America—Southcom—and the turnover of the canal at the end of 1999 seemed to close a chapter on the relationship. However, economic interests of other countries mean that Panama will not again revert to a "backwater" country. Though U.S. dependence on the canal has declined, other countries are even more dependent on its continued function, particularly those in Asia and western South America. Japan has depended heavily on the canal. True to its long-term planning tradition, China began developing a trading relationship with Panama in the mid-1980s during the buildup of the Noriega crisis. In concert with Chinese investors, the canal is undergoing a $1 billion modernization program, which includes doubling the width of Gaillard Cut and the construction of a third set of locks.

Panama's southern border with Colombia is still one of the most volatile in Latin America, which has prompted what some charge is a "remilitarization" of Panamanian security forces. A 2005 study by the Center for International Policy shows that Panama, which has no army, received a huge increase in US military training—from 25 policemen trained in 2002 to more than 900 last year. In Latin America, only Colombia and Bolivia had more soldiers trained by the United States in 2003.

At the cusp of the twenty-first century, Panama faces a generational challenge to solidify its democracy, secure its borders within a peaceful, non-military framework, and improve the economic lot of a large portion of its population. General Torrijos once said that he did not want enter into history, but into the canal. But with the canal now a completely Panamanian waterway, Panama is assuming its rights and responsibilities as a truly sovereign state as it enters into the next phase of its history.

NOTES

1. Organization of American States, Inter-American Commission on Human Rights, *Annual Report of the Inter-American Commission on Human Rights: 1990–1991* (Washington, D.C., 1991).

2. Anthony Gray and Maxwell Manwaring, "Operation Just Cause" in Robert B. Oakley, et al., *Policing the New World Disorder: Peace Operations and Public Security* (Washington, D.C.: National Defense University Press, 1998).

3. The Miami Herald, "The Panama Canal: Countdown to 1999," December 27, 1991.

4. William Furlong, "Panama: The Difficult Transition Toward Democracy," *Journal of Interamerican Studies and World Affairs* 35, no. 3 (Autumn 1993): 22.

5. Margaret Scranton, "Consolidation after Imposition: Panama's 1992 Referendum," *Journal of Interamerican Studies and World Affairs* 35, no. 3 (Autumn 1993): 88.

6. Orlando J. Pérez, "Public Opinion and the Future of U.S.-Panama Relations, *Journal of Interamerican Studies and World Affairs* 41, no. 3 (Autumn 1999): 5.

7. Margaret Scranton, "Panama's First Post-Invasion Election," *Journal of Interamerican Studies and World Affairs* 37, no. 1 (Spring 1995): 71.

8. Robert C. Harding II, *Military Foundations of Panamanian Politics* (Brunswick, NJ: Transaction Publishing, 2001), 186.

9. Marcos Gandásegui, "The 1998 Referendum in Panama: A Popular Vote Against Neoliberalism," *Latin American Perspectives* 26, no. 2 (March 1999): 162.

10. Amnesty International, "Panama/Colombia: Rights of Refugees to Escape from Death," Amnesty International Report 44, no. 6 (June 1, 1997).

11. John Lindsay-Poland, *Emperor in the Jungle: The Hidden History of the U.S. in Panama* (Durham, NC: Duke University Press, 2003), 141.

12. Robert Pastor, quoted in "No Home on Panama's Range," *The Washington Post*, January 10, 2000: A14.

13. Orlando J. Pérez, "Public Opinion and the Future of U.S.-Panama Relations," *Journal of Interamerican Studies and World Affairs* 41 no. 3 (Fall 1999): 10.

14. "Freedom In the World 2006," www.freedomhouse.org.

Notable People in the History of Panama

Amador Guerrero, Manuel (1833–1909). He was the first president of Panama and was a founding father of Panamanian independence from Colombia.

Arango, José Agustín (1841–1909). Originally Panama's representative in the Colombian Senate, he became one of Panama's founding fathers. For one year after independence (1903–1904), he served as president of the postindependence provisional junta.

Ardito Barletta, Nicolás "Nikki" (1938–). A former vice president of the World Bank and former president of the Latin American Export Bank, he was elected as president in 1984 in Panama's first direct (though fraudulent) elections following the 1968 coup. He was a figurehead leader for Manuel Noriega and was replaced a year later when he attempted to force Noriega's resignation. In 1993 he became the head of a Panama Canal transition group, the Interoceanic Region Authority.

Arias Calderón, Ricardo (1930?–). A former university professor, he was exiled by the military dictatorship from 1969 to 1978. He ran for first vice president in 1989 and won. In the latter half of the 1990s he was president of Christian Democrat International, a global group dedicated to promoting Christian democracy.

Arias Madrid, Arnulfo (1901–1988). He was easily Panama's most visible politician. He ran for president multiple times and won three times, frequently vacillating between ideological extremes and using extreme nationalism to further his causes. In each instance, however, he was overthrown by Panama's military. He is the namesake of the Arnulfista Party, which was founded two years after his death.

Arias Madrid, Harmodio (1886–1962). The older brother of Arnulfo Arias, he was one of the leaders of the revolutionary movement in 1931 that overthrew the government of Florencio Harmodio Arosemena. He served as president from 1932 to 1936. He is recognized as the first Latin American leader to hold press conferences, and the Universidad de Panama was founded under his administration.

Arosemena Quinzada, Alcibíades (1883–1958). A member of one of Panama's most influential families, he ran as a vice presidential candidate with Arnulfo Arias in 1948, and after Arias's impeachment in 1951, Arosemena served as president for the remainder of the term (to 1952).

Arosemena Guillén, Florencio Harmodio (1872–1945). He was elected president in 1928 and served until 1931, when he was overthrown in a coup by the Arias brothers' Acción Comunal.

Arosemena Barreati, Juan Demóstenes (1879–1939). He was elected president in 1936 as a coalition candidate of the National Revolutionary, National Liberal, and Conservative parties. He was responsible for pushing a nonintervention policy on the United States with regards to Panama. He died in office.

Arosemena, Pablo (1836–). Member of the first post-independence provisional junta, he served as president from 1910–1912 after the death in office of President de Obaldía.

Aspinwall, William Henry (1807–1875). He was an American entrepreneur who headed the effort that built the trans-Panama railroad, which opened in 1855. The city of Colón was originally called Aspinwall in his honor.

Blades, Rubén (1948–). While originally gaining fame as salsa singer with a social message, Blades later became known as a political figure in Panama when he formed a political party, Papa Egora, and then ran for president in 1994, placing third. He is a graduate of law from the Universidad de Panamá and holds a master's degree in international law from Harvard University. He was appointed Panama's Minister of Tourism in 2004.

Boyd, Aquilino (1921–). He has been one of Panama's most active diplomats. He twice served as Panama's Foreign Minister and was a principal negotiator in the Panama Canal Treaties of 1977. He served as Panama's ambassador to Mexico and the United Kingdom, and in 1997 he became Panama's permanent representative to the United Nations.

Boyd, Archibald (1827–). He was a American immigrant in Panama who founded the country's first newspaper, the English-language *Star and Herald* in 1852. One of his sons, Federico, would be a founding member of independent Panama.

Boyd, Augusto Samuel (1879–1957). The son of Federico Boyd, he was vice president from 1936 to 1939 and served briefly as president from 1939 to 1940.

Boyd, Federico Augusto (1851–1924). He was the son of Archibald Boyd, and was a member of the revolutionary junta of independent Panama in 1903. He served very briefly as president in 1910 and also served as Panama's ambassador to the United States.

Bunau-Varilla, Phillipe (1859–1940). He was Lesseps's chief engineer during the French canal construction attempt. After the French failure, he was instrumental in persuading the United States to support Panama's move toward independence. After Panama's declaration of independence, he acted as Panama's agent to the United States and signed the original canal treaty agreement for Panama that permitted the United States to begin construction of the canal.

Cipriano Mosquera, Tomás (1798–1878). He was the president of Colombia who gave transit rights through Panama to the United States. This agreement laid the foundation for the Panama Railroad.

Colón, Bartolomé (1437–1514). He was the elder brother of Cristóbal Colón (Christopher Columbus) and founder of the first Spanish settlement in Panama called Santa María de Belén. However, his attempt to subdue the Indians caused the settlement's destruction.

Colón, Cristóbal (1451–1506). Known as Christopher Columbus in English, Colón was an Genovese navigator who landed in Panama in 1502 during his final voyage to the New World. He left his brother, Bartolomé, to found the first Spanish settlement in Panama.

Cromwell, William Nelson (1854–1948): He was a New York attorney who lobbied Congress for the bankrupt French canal company in its efforts to get U.S. support for the project. Along with Phillipe Bunau-Varilla, Cromwell was instrumental in persuading the U.S. government to choose Panama as the site of the canal.

De la Guardia Navarro, Ernesto (1904–1983). He was elected president in 1956. A more conservative member of the oligarchy, he reduced many of Remón's social programs.

De la Guardia Arango, Ricardo Adolfo (1899–1969). He was president of Panama from 1941 to 1945, replacing Arnulfo Arias after the latter's overthrow. He was notable for his cooperation with the United States during World War II, allowing substantial U.S. military buildup in Panama. He himself was forced out of office in 1945.

De Lesseps, Ferdinand Marie (1805–1894). He was the French financier of the Suez Canal who began construction of the Panama Canal in 1881. When the canal project failed, his company went bankrupt, producing one of France's largest financial fiascos of the time.

De Obaldía, José Domingo (1845–1910). He was a Colombian official who defected to the Panamanian revolutionaries' cause. He was elected president in 1908 and served until his death in office in 1910.

Díaz Arosemena, Domingo (1875–1949). He became president in 1948 after a fraudulent election against Arnulfo Arias. He died in office the next year.

Endara Galimany, Guillermo (1936–). He headed the presidential ticket that challenged Noriega's dictatorship in 1989. He was installed as president on a U.S. military base hours before the invasion of Panama. He was president from 1989 to 1994.

Ford Boyd, Guillermo (1930?–). Affectionately known as "Billy," he was the candidate for second vice president who in 1989 became world famous for being beaten on television by Noriega's "dignity battalions." Since 1999, he has served as Panama's Ambassador to the United States.

Goethals, George Washington (1858–1928). He was a United States military engineer who was appointed by Roosevelt as chief engineer of the Isthmian Canal Commission, which directed the U.S. effort to complete the Panama Canal. He is credited with many engineering feats that made the canal possible, including the creation of Lake Gatún. He served as governor of the Canal Zone from 1914 to 1917.

González, Rodrigo "Rory" (1935?–). A very close friend of Omar Torrijos, he was instrumental in the founding of the Partido Revolucionario Democrático.

Gorgas, William Crawford (1854–1920). A U.S. army surgeon, he learned about mosquitoes' role in malaria transmission from a Cuban doctor while stationed in Cuba. After his transfer to Panama, he implemented far-reaching sanitation programs that virtually eliminated malaria in the Canal Zone.

Herrera, Tomás (1800–1854). Originally a Colombian governor of Panama, he became a revered national hero who led the first unsuccessful independence movement. The Panamanian providence of Herrera is named for him.

Mahan, Alfred Thayer (1840–1914). He was the American military strategist whose "two-ocean" doctrine following the Spanish-American War of 1889 assured the construction of a trans-isthmus waterway.

Morgan, Henry (1635–1688). He was the English buccaneer who raided the first site of Panama City in 1671, sacking and burning it to the ground. After this destruction, Panama City was rebuilt at its present location.

Noriega, Manuel Antonio (1936–). He became a CIA-recruited spy during his military school days. Under Omar Torrijos, he was made the head of Panama's intelligence agency, the G-2. After Torrijos's death, he ruled Panama as absolute dictator until the U.S. invasion in December, 1989. He was arrested by the United States and sentenced by a Florida court to 30 years in prison.

Núñez de Balboa, Vasco (1475–1519). He was the mayor of Panama's first permanent settlement, Santa María de La Antigua del Darién. He led a contingent of soldiers through the Panamanian jungle to become the first European to see the Pacific from Latin America. He was falsely accused of treason by Panama's new governor and executed.

Moscoso Rodríguez de Arias, Mireya Elisa (1940–). She is the widow of former Panamanian president Arnulfo Arias, who she married while the two were in exile in Miami after Arias's 1968 overthrow. She became Panama's first female president in 1999 and oversaw the assumption of the Panama Canal at the end of 1999.

Moss, Ambler (1938?–). He was a member of the U.S. contingent that negotiated the Panama Canal Treaties in 1977. He then served as U.S.

ambassador to Panama from 1978 to 1982, and he twice served on the U.S.-Panama Consultative Committee. He was the founding director of the University of Miami's North-South Center.

Paredes, Rubén Darío (1940?–). A member of the military junta that overthrew Arias in 1968, he briefly ruled (1982–1983) Panama until he was ousted by Noriega.

Pérez Balladares, Ernesto (1946–). Nicknamed "Toro" (Bull), he was a Torrijos protégé who ran successfully for president in 1994. He presided over Panama's preparations for the handover of the canal, but he was unsuccessful in his referendum attempt to allow Panamanian presidents to run for reelection.

Remón Cantera, José Antonio (1908–1955). He was the first Panamanian to head the National Police. He resigned from the police and ran for president as a civilian, winning in 1952. During his administration, Panama obtained important amendments to the Panama Canal treaty, particularly a 250 percent increase in the annuity. He also changed the name of the military from the National Police to the National Guard. He was largely responsible for the inclusion of mestizos into the force. He was assassinated while attending horse races.

Royo Sánchez, Arístides (1940–). An attorney, he was appointed president in 1978 by Omar Torrijos and was ousted by the National Guard in 1982. He later became Panama's Ambassador to the United States.

Torrijos Espino, Martín Erasto (1963–). He is the son of former dictator, Omar Torrijos. After completing his education in the United States, he returned to Panama and first ran unsuccessfully for president in 1999, then successfully in 2004 as the PRD candidate.

Torrijos Herrera, Omar Efraín (1929–1981). He was a mestizo who rose through the ranks of the Panamanian National Guard to become dictator of Panama in 1968. He is credited with having fundamentally reformed the country's social system, turning it away from elite domination. He died in a plane crash in western Panama in 1981.

Bibliographic Essay

Early Histories

Histories of Panama that focus largely on the pre-independence period include David Howarth, *Panama: Four Hundred Years of Dreams and Cruelty* (New York: McGraw-Hill, 1966), an excellent study that spans the early period from colonization to the building of the canal. E. Taylor Parks, *Colombia and the United States, 1765–1934* (New York: Ayer County Publications, 1970) provides valuable insight into Panama when it was a province of Colombia. Ricaurte Soler, *Formas ideológicas de la Nación Panameña* (San José, Costa Rica: Editorial Universitaria Centroamericana, 1972) gives an exceptional overview of the formation of Panamanian nationalism. Other works include Dwight C. Miner, "The Fight for the Panama Canal Route: The Story of the Spooner Act and the Hay-Herran Treaty," *American Historical Review* 46, no. 2, (January 1941): 437–438; Peter Earle, *The Sack of Panamá: Sir Henry Morgan's Adventures on the Spanish Main* (New York: Viking Press, 1982); and Bonifacio J. Pereira, *Historia de Panamá* (Panama City: Editorial Litográphico, 1969).

Building the Road and the Canal

Among the books that chronicle the building of the Panama Railroad and early searches for a canal, perhaps the most comprehensive and detailed is David McCullough, *Path between the Seas: The Creation of the Panama Canal, 1870–1914* (New York: Simon & Schuster, 1978), which chronicles in detail the circumstances, people, and events that led to the canal's eventual construction. Other important works Joseph L Schott, *The Story of the Building of the Panama Railroad, 1849–1855* (Indianapolis: Bobbs-Merrill, 1967); Todd Balf, *The Darkest Jungle: The True Story of the Darien Expedition and America's Ill-Fated Race to Connect the Seas* (New York: Crown, 2003); Michael LaRosa and Germán Mejía, *The United States Discovers Panama: The Writings of Soldiers, Scholars, and Scoundrels, 1850–1905* (New York: Rowman & Littlefield Publishers, 2004); Gerstle Mack, *The Land Divided: A History of the Panama Canal & Other Isthmian Canal Projects* (New York: Alfred A. Knopf, 1944); Joseph B. Bishop, *The Panama Gateway* (New York: Charles Scribner's, Sons. 1915); Ira Bennett, *History of the Panama Canal* (Washington, D.C.: Historical Publishing Co., 1915); D. G. Payne, *The Impossible Dream* (New York: William Morrow & Co, Inc., 1972); Donald Chidsey, *The Panama Canal, An Informal History of its Concept, Building, and Present Status* (New York: Crown Publishers, Inc., 1970); Lancelot S. Lewis, *The West Indian in Panama: Black Labor in Panama, 1850–1914* (Lanham, MD: University Press of America, 1980); and Joseph L. Scott, *Rails across Panama; The Story of the Building of the Panama Railroad, 1849–1855.* (Indianapolis: Bobbs-Merrill, 1967). Harry Franck, *Zone Policeman 88* (Manchester, NH: Ayer Company Publishers, 1970) is a fascinating account of day-to-day life during the canal's construction. A newer work, Ovidio Díaz Espino, *How Wall Street Created a Nation: J.P. Morgan, Teddy Roosevelt, and the Panama Canal* (New York: Four Walls Eight Windows, 2003), adds to the canal story by highlighting the role of Wall Street financiers in promoting the canal-building project. Harmodio Arias, *The Panama Canal: A Study in International Law and Diplomacy* (New York: Arno Press, 1970) is invaluable as an educated Panamanian insider's view of the acquisition and building of the canal. Others include G. W. Goethals, *The Panama Canal: An Engineering Treatise* (1916); M. P. DuVal, *And the Mountains Will Move* (1947, reprint, Greenwood Press, 1968); J. P. Speller, *The Panama Canal* (1972); and Alfred Charles Richard, *The Panama Canal in American National Consciousness, 1870–1990* (New York: Taylor & Francis, 1990).

U.S.-Panama Relations

A number of books focus specifically on the history of the special relationship between Panama and the United States and the latter's role in the former's politics and society: David N. Farnsworth and James W. McKinney, *U.S.-Panama Relations, 1903–1978: A Study in Linkage Politics* (Boulder, CO: Westview Press, 1983); Richard H. Collin, *Theodore Roosevelt's Caribbean: The Panama Canal, the Monroe Doctrine, and the Latin American Context* (Baton Rouge: Louisiana State University, 1990), a is superb accounting of early twentieth-century U.S. foreign policy, in which Panama figured highly; Edward F. Dolan, *Panama and the United States: Their Canal, Their Stormy Years* (New York: Franklin Watts, 1990); Michael L. Conniff, *Panama and the United States: The Forced Alliance* (Athens: University of Georgia Press, 1992), a concise and insightful review of the relationship; John Weeks and Phil Gunson, *Panama: Made in the USA* (London: Latin American Bureau, 1991); John Major, *Prize Possession: The United States Government and the Panama Canal 1903–1979* (London: Cambridge University Press, 1993); and John Lindsay-Poland, *Emperors in the Jungle: The Hidden History of the U.S. in Panama* (Durham, NC: Duke University Press, 2003), distinctive for its study of the human and environmental costs of the long U.S. presence around the Panama Canal. Mark Falcoff, *Panama's Canal: What Happens When the United States Gives a Small Country What It Wants* (Washington, D.C.: AEI Press, 1998) provides a critical analysis of the handover of the canal. John Major, *Prize Possession: The United States Government and the Panama Canal 1903–1979* (New York: Cambridge University Press, 2003) is a comprehensive history of the Panama Canal, explicating the U.S. administration and the role of the Panama Canal within the context of Panama as well as U.S. intervention in Panamanian politics.

Military in Politics

A small collection of books exclusively studies Panama's military in national politics. Larry LaRae Pippin, *The Remón Era: An Analysis of a Decade of Events in Panama, 1947–1957* (Institute of Hispanic American and Luso-Brazilian Studies, Stanford University, 1964); Renato Pereira, *Panama: fuerzas armadas y política* (Panama City: Ediciones Nueva Universidad, 1979); Steve C. Ropp, *Panamanian Politics: From Guarded Nation to National Guard* (New York: Praeger Publishers, 1982); George A. Priestley, *Military Government and Popular Participation in Panama: The Torrijos Regime 1968–1975* (Boulder, CO: Westview Press, 1986); Carlos Guevara Mann, *Panamanian Militarism: A Historical Interpretation* (Athens: Ohio University Press, 1996); Thomas L. Pearcy, *We Answer Only to God: Politics and the Military in Panama, 1903–1947* (Albuquerque: University of New Mexico Press, 1998); Robert C. Harding II, *Military Foundations of Panamanian Politics* (Somerset, NJ: Transaction Publishers, 2001).

Economic Development

A few books focus exclusively on Panama's economic development. Andrew Zimbalist and John Weeks, *Panama at the Crossroads: Economic Development and Political Change in the Twentieth Century* (Berkeley: University of California Press, 1991) is the most comprehensive. Also of interest are Robert E. Looney, *The Economic Development of Panama: The Impact of World Inflation on an Open Economy* (New York: Praeger, 1976) and William C. Merrill, *Panama's Economic Development: The Role of Agriculture* (Ames: Iowa State University Press, 1975).

Panama Canal Treaties

Books on the period surrounding the Panama Canal treaties negotiations include William J. Jorden, *Panama Odyssey* (Austin: University of Texas Press, 1984), a hefty tome that chronicles in minute detail both American and Panamanian diplomatic negotiations and maneuvers; William L. Furlong and Margaret E. Scranton, *The Dynamics of Foreign Policymaking: The President, the Congress, and the Panama Canal Treaties* (Boulder, CO: Westview Press, 1984); Alfred Charles Richard Jr., *The Panama Canal in American National Consciousness, 1870–1990* (New York: Garland Publishing, Inc., 1990); Sheldon B. Liss, *The Canal: Aspects of United States–Panamanian Relations* (South Bend, IA: Notre Dame University Press, 1967); Denison Kitchel, *The Truth about the Panama Canal* (New Rochelle, NY: Arlington House, 1978); George D. Moffet, *The Limits of Victory: The Ratification of the Panama Canal Treaties* (Ithaca, NY: Cornell University Press, 1985); former U.S. president Jimmy Carter, *Keeping the Faith: Memoirs of a President* (New York: Bantam Books, 1982); and G. H. Summ and T. Kelly, *The Good Neighbors: America, Panama, and the 1977 Canal Treaties* (Athens: Ohio University Press, 1988).

Years of Dictatorship and the Invasion

Some of the most robust literature on Panama examines the 1968–1990 period of military dictatorship. Daniel Goldrich, *Sons of the Establishment: Elite Youth in Panama* (Chicago, 1966) is the only such study published; Walter LaFeber, *The Panama Canal: The Crisis in Historical Perspective*, updated ed. (New York: Oxford University Press, 1989), perhaps the most satisfying history of Panama, masterfully crafts a picture of a country continuously under the influence of outside actors. Richard M. Koster and Guillermo Sanchez, *In the Time of Tyrants: Panama: 1968–1990* chronicles the entire period of military dictatorship, emphasizing especially some of the more torrid aspects of Noriega's tenure and the society. John Dinges, *Our Man in Panama* (New York: Random House, 1990) utilizes previously classified documents, supplemented by congressional hearings and interviews, to provide a fascinating insight into Noriega's rise to power. Frederick Kempe, *Divorcing the Dictator* (New York: Putnam Publishing, 1990) provides similar information but emphasizes more the CIA's role in promoting the Noriega dictatorship and also covers the 1989 U.S. invasion and its aftermath.

Other notable books include Kevin Buckley, *Panama: The Whole Story* (New York: Simon & Schuster, 1991); Thomas Donnelly, Margaret Roth, and Caleb Baker, *Operation Just Cause: The Storming of Panama* (New York: Lexington Books, 1991); Tom Barry, John Lindsay-Poland, Marco Gandásegui, and Peter Simonson, *Inside Panama* (Washington, D.C.: Resource Center Press, 1995); Maron J. Simon, *The Panama Affair* (New York: Scribner, 1971); George Priestly, *Military Government and Popular Participation in Panama: The Torrijos Regime, 1968–1975* (Boulder, CO: Westview Press, 1986); Omar Torrijos, *Imagen y voz* (Panama: Centro de Estudios Torrijistas, 1985), the general's own account of his dictatorship; Graham Greene, *Getting to Know the General* (New York: Thorndike Press, 1984); and Luis E. Murillo, *The Noriega Mess: The Drugs, The Canal and Why America Invaded* (Berkeley, CA: Video Books, 1995). Manuel Noriega and Peter Eisner, *America, Prisoner: The Memoirs of Manuel Noriega* (New York: Random House, 1997) is Noriega's first-person story of his relationship with the United States and why he was captured.

A number of fine Panamanian sources recount the period of dictatorship: Omar Torrijos Herrera, *Papeles del General* (Madrid: Centro de Estudios Torrijistas, 1984), a justification by the general himself of the dictatorship and José Agustín Catalá, *Panamá: autodeterminación contra intervención de Estados Unidos* (Caracas: Ediciones Centauro, 1989). Ricaurte Soler, *Panamá: historia de una crisis* (Mexico City: Siglo Veintiuno Editores, S.A. de C.V., 1989) is an intriguing, penetrating analysis of the 1970–1989 period by Panama's preeminent modern historian; Juan B. Sosa, *In Defiance: The Battle Against General Noriega Fought from Panama's Embassy in Washington* (Washington, D.C.: Francis Press, 1999) is an interesting memoir of Panama's ambassador to the United States who fought against Noriega's attempt to wrest control of the embassy from him. Thomas Donnelly, Margaret Roth, and Caleb Baker, *Operation Just Cause: The Storming of Panama* (New York: Lexington Books, 1991) is a minutely detailed and definitive retelling of the invasion based on hundreds of interviews. Other works on the invasion include Malcolm McConnell, *Just Cause: The Real Story of America's High-Tech Invasion of Panama* (New York: St. Martin's Press, 1991); and Bruce W. Watson and Peter Tsouras, eds., *Operation Just Cause: The U.S. Intervention in Panama* (Boulder, CO: Westview Press, 1991).

Index

About the Author

ROBERT C. HARDING is Chair and Assistant Professor of International Relations at Lynchburg College (Virginia). His research interests are democratization, civil-military relations, and environmental policymaking in Latin America.

Other Titles in the Greenwood Histories of the Modern Nations
Frank W. Thackeray and John E. Findling, Series Editors

The History of Argentina
Daniel K. Lewis

The History of Australia
Frank G. Clarke

The History of the Baltic States
Kevin O'Connor

The History of Brazil
Robert M. Levine

The History of Canada
Scott W. See

The History of Central America
Thomas Pearcy

The History of Chile
John L. Rector

The History of China
David C. Wright

The History of Congo
Didier Gondola

The History of Cuba
Clifford L. Staten

The History of Egypt
Glenn E. Perry

The History of France
W. Scott Haine

The History of Germany
Eleanor L. Turk

The History of Ghana
Roger S. Gocking

The History of Great Britain
Anne Baltz Rodrick

The History of Holland
Mark T. Hooker

The History of India
John McLeod

The History of Indonesia
Steven Drakeley

The History of Iran
Elton L. Daniel

The History of Iraq
Courtney Hunt

The History of Ireland
Daniel Webster Hollis III

The History of Israel
Arnold Blumberg

The History of Italy
Charles L. Killinger

The History of Japan
Louis G. Perez

The History of Korea
Djun Kil Kim

The History of Mexico
Burton Kirkwood

The History of New Zealand
Tom Brooking

The History of Nigeria
Toyin Falola

The History of Poland
M.B. Biskupski

The History of Portugal
James M. Anderson